Bro ther angelo

COOKING WITH
CRAZY CHARLEY IV

Great Cooking

Charley

D0018929

COOKING WITH CRAZY CHARLEY IV
Cajun and Creole Cuisine

Charley and Ruth Addison
Foreword by Julius Champagne

PELICAN PUBLISHING COMPANY
Gretna 2006

Copyright © 1998, 2000, 2003, 2006
By Charley Addison and Ruth Addison
All rights reserved

First edition, 1998
Second edition, 2000
Third edition, 2003
First Pelican edition, 2006

The word "Pelican" and the depiction of a pelican
are trademarks of Pelican Publishing Company, Inc.,
and are registered in the U.S. Patent and Trademark Office.

Library of Congress Cataloging-in-Publication Data

Addison, Charley.
    Cooking with Crazy Charley IV : Cajun and Creole
cuisine / Charley and Ruth Addison ; foreword by Julius
Champagne.— 1st Pelican ed.
          p. cm.
    Includes bibliographical references and index.
    ISBN-13: 978-1-58980-387-9 (pbk. : alk. paper)
    1. Cookery, American—Louisiana style. 2. Cookery, Creole.
3. Cookery, Cajun. I. Title: Cooking with Crazy Charley 4. II.
Title: Cooking with Crazy Charley four. III. Addison, Ruth. IV.
Title.
    TX715.2.L68A35 2006
    641.59763—dc22

                                                2005035828

Printed in the United States of America

Published by Pelican Publishing Company, Inc.
1000 Burmaster Street, Gretna, Louisiana 70053

CONTENTS

FOREWORD

Charley Addison has always been in the midst of, or on the fringe of, Cajun culture. He has been a keen student of Cajun folk ways. The mores, point of view, and style of Cajun living have always been deep in his affections.

His earliest contact was with a member of his own community referred to as the "Crazy Cajun" (because of that individual's different mode of living). From this early contact onward, through his days at L.S.U. and beyond, Charley 's love of Cajun culture steadily grew. His contacts in the Cajun country became more frequent and broad.

His deep and abiding interest in everything Cajun, in particular, its cuisine, has resulted in a special avocation for him. He is an unofficial, but unabashed promoter of Cajun culture and of Cajun country, which he sometimes refers to as "God's Country."

The Cajun people have responded to him in a like manner, with much affection.

The Cajun-way, as it is sometimes referred to, includes good food, tall tales, danceable music, good-fellowship, a relaxed attitude toward time constraints, a distaste for supervision of any kind, occasional piety, live-and-let-live attitude, and a fascination with politics, football, and pretty women. Cajun women take a sterner attitude toward life, are less fascinated by football, politics, and would like their men to be more dedicated.

Feature events occurring in Cajun country are the food festivals. These usually include performance by a Cajun band. Regrettably, too often nowadays, the music, though danceable, is not authentic Cajun music. It is now necessary to search for the unadulterated variety, which is not as widely performed as it once was, but we're working on it. *"So hurrae down befo's all you to gon."*

This book reminds one of Jean Pierre's dream. Long ago in Nova Scotia Jean Pierre had a dream about the future. He dreamt that British soldiers were burning his house and barns. He and his family were being moved at gunpoint and loaded like cattle aboard an awaiting ship.

Once he and his family and neighbors were boarded, the ship set sail and in a southerly direction. It sailed for many days until it reached a small city located alongside a deep and wide river.

The ship anchored there for several days while officials made arrangements concerning the passengers who were subsequently transferred to another vessel.

This boat then traveled up-river several miles and then off-loaded its human cargo on the west bank, later known as the Acadian Coast.

Some of the people settled in the immediate environment and some traveled inland. They fanned out in all directions.

These original pioneers and their descendants cleared the wilderness, built homes, held fais-do-dos (pronounced faye-doe-doe and meaning party time, dance time, storytelling time, all in one), attended church, held Mardi Gras, developed food festivals and other social-cultural events.

The life of these descendants was centered on the pleasure of living. Work was tolerated, but only occasionally enjoyed. Personal independence from strictures, the domination by bosses and other authority figures (even religious ones) was highly prized.

Jean Pierre was deep into his dream. He was at a fais-do-do and enjoying himself tremendously when, within his dream, some rude fellow came up to him and said, "Mais, wake up Jean Pierre. You not in Paradise, mon. You jus dreamin'."

This book is like Jean Pierre's dream. It's got everything in it—a buffet of Cajun culture.

Julius Champagne

ACKNOWLEDGMENTS

Thanks to all of our wonderful customers who enjoy our authentic Cajun and Creole products and share recipes they have created using Crazy Charley Sauces. Many of these recipes will be found in this book. Credit has been given to customers who have submitted their recipes. Keep sending your recipes. We know that our sauces can be used in ways only your imaginations and taste buds can create.

A special thanks to Paul Strazzullo, our "cooker," who has advised us, hung in there with us when the going got tough, and has become a trusted friend over the years.

Thank you Wendy Eidson for the clever drawings you made of our products for Mo Hotta Mo Betta Mail order catalog and for this book.

Friends are wonderful at times like these. Joanne Ryno you encouraged me with your critique, proofing and suggestions. Thanks to my grandson, Tyler Wedan, for sharing his knowledge on the computer to help me get this book ready for publication.

Many thanks to our customers for the letters you write and the emergency calls you make when you are unable to find your favorite product. Thank you so much!

Photo by Shmuel Thaler

INTRODUCTION

The only thing more important to me on this Earth than food is my wife. Her nickname is "Monk" because she jumps around like a monkey, rarely sitting still.

The recipes she put in this book are tried and true. Cook them and you'll dazzle your family and friends with food fit for a king.

I have loved to cook since I was nine, when my grandmother taught me to fry Johnny cakes. Being from my part of the country has allowed me to experience the best of foods. Louisiana and Southern cooking is becoming a very popular cuisine.

I often start a cooking show with this joke—"Hello, y'all. I'm happy to see you. I'm honored to know the three best Cajun chefs in the world. The other two are Paul Prudhomme and Emeril."

Sincerely, folks, you will love the recipes in this cookbook my wife has put together and you will use them over and over again, I guarantee! Bon appetit.

This book is also about a people and a place I have loved all my life, and I want to share it with you.

I have traveled extensively all over this varied world of ours. I can say without reservation that the "Cajun" folk of south Louisiana are the happiest, friendliest, most interesting, and most fun-loving people I have ever encountered. They have a passion for life that is special, a respect for life that is wonderful, and a love of life that is pure.

The culinary delights of south Louisiana are unusual in all the world. Food is always of paramount importance in homes there and at all social affairs.

Chefs Paul Prudhomme and Justin Wilson caused foods like jambalaya, gumbo, crawfish and blackened everything to appear on menus throughout the world. Cajun food is the rage and will stay in vogue because it's so darn good.

Many people tend to get "Cajun" and "Creole" mixed up. They have similarities, true, but they are very different people and have different cultures and food.

The Cajun people are, contrary to some portraits, usually hardworking, thrifty, family-oriented people. They are not as some outsiders try to portray them—little, dark, uneducated, heavy-drinking fools. Folks, these people are so proud, they receive less public support than any other group of people in the United States. I know Cajuns who would not even accept unemployment payments because they thought it too similar to welfare. And you will not find greater patriotism anywhere in the country.

Cajuns, and their cooking, tend to be "country." Cajuns descended from the old French Normans and Huguenots.

Creoles are a mixture of French, Spanish and West Indian people, with roots in New Orleans. Their cuisine is city cooking with the fancy sauces and "haute" presentation.

Most people think all Cajun food is hot. Not so. Our food is well seasoned but not necessarily hot. Of course, if it is not hot enough, there is always that old faithful bottle of Tabasco nearby, which can take care of the problem.

Cajun heat is meant to accent the flavor of food, not cover it up. If the food is so hot that all you can taste is the heat, then it is either poor Cajun cooking or an imitation that one must watch out for.

Now sit back and browse through this work. Use it as a travel guide through Cajun country. Use the gourmet and country recipes to experience south Louisiana cuisine that is nothing short of magic. Pause and smell the magnolias.

Charley

Charley introduced me to the flavors of Cajun and Creole foods many years ago when we were dating. He wooed me with good food and flowers. He tells people I was born in Kansas, where we never used seasonings. We used salt, black pepper, sage, cinnamon, and nutmeg. I cannot remember any other spices or herbs in our home. Spicy or not, I love to cook. My mother was confined to bed for a year when I was 8, so I became the cook for our family of 5. I wore a path between the kitchen and bedroom asking my mother, "What do I do next?" I have been asking ever since.

I have written parts of this book to share the many quick, easy, and delicious recipes I've learned by watching and asking Charley, "What do I do next?" I have learned to cook with sauces as the stimulus for flavor, and even to enjoy a bit of spicy sizzle. Thank you, Charley. You are not crazy after all.

Love ya! Ruth

HOW "CRAZY CAJUN" GOT ITS NAME

There was an old Cajun who lived in my hometown named Oscar. He lived in a small shack he built by himself out by the river, on the edge of the swamp.

Oscar had a pet llama that he fed chewing tobacco to who would spit at anyone who came near. The llama was Oscar's companion, pet and beast of burden.

When I was a kid I used to go by Oscar's cabin after I finished my paper route if I had an extra paper. I would give Oscar the paper and sit on his steps and ask him to tell me some of his fantastic stories.

I sat enthralled as Oscar spun tales about the night creatures, the screaming Banshees, wild ghosts and goblins that devoured lost children, alligator Gars that were 10 feet long and had legs to climb upon the bank of the bayou at night and could eat a man whole, and the old haints that roamed the swamp looking for human bodies to take over.

I spent as much time with Oscar as I could. He taught me to fish, find the best catfish holes, track animals, to be invisible in the swamp so the squirrels, rabbits and deer would walk right up to me. I loved Oscar.

Like so many people that are different he was viewed with, distrust and fear by the "regular" people. He would only come to town about once a month with his pet to buy the few supplies he needed. Oscar was made fun of and laughed at by people and they called him "That Crazy Cajun." I named my company after that old "Crazy Cajun." I loved that old man.

Charley

COOKING WITH
CRAZY CHARLEY IV

A "CAJUN COUNTRY" EXPERIENCE

The foods of Cajun country are simply wonderful, a special eating experience known only to those who partake. But the food is only part of the whole that makes the Cajun country experience so unique.

My husband, Charley, has experienced Cajun country since birth. He grew up with gumbo, jambalaya, boudin, wild game, fish and seafood, swamps, and bayous.

Charley introduced me to Louisiana over thirty years ago. We spend time there every year, eating and enjoying this unique area and visiting family in Thibodaux. I was born in Kansas and raised in California and Oregon. Going to the South was like entering a new world with its unfamiliar sights, sounds, and flavors. With these visits to Cajun country and New Orleans, I have caught the essence of Louisiana as an "outlander".

Being in Cajun country is a multifarious experience. The Cajun people are fun loving and friendly. I felt like a stranger until I looked into their faces and saw the smiles of welcome. It compelled me to see more of these people and where they live, work, and play. You, too, can catch the essence of Cajun country, in Southwest Louisiana.

Baton Rouge, the Louisiana state capital, is a city where you can see and feel the colorful history of the state. Visit the new capitol building, the tallest capital building in the United States. From the top, you can see for miles along the Mississippi River. Contrast the new with a visit to the historical old capital building. You can take a peek at yesteryear at Magnolia Mound or Rural Life Museum, tour over 20 elegantly restored antebellum homes, and feel the spirit of the Tigers with a visit to Louisiana State University (LSU). Charley attended this great university back in the 50s. You can enjoy Cajun and Creole foods at Cafe Louisiana on Acadian Thruway or zip over to I-10 and Bluebonnet Road exit to Mulate's Cajun restaurant. Catch the music of a great Cajun Band, devour mounds of catfish, gumbo, jambalaya, Crawfish Etouffee, and watch local Cajuns dance.

Drive west on I-10 from Baton Rouge deeper into Southwest Louisiana, which makes up Cajun country. Cross the Atchafalaya Swamp that seems to go on forever. About halfway across, Charley laughed as I insisted upon stopping at a turn out so I could just feast my "outlander" eyes on the vastness of this enchanting swampland.

Drive on west to Henderson where Pat Huval has operated his Cajun seafood restaurant business since 1952. One of the first Cajun restaurants that became known for superb Cajun cooking.

Stop in Breaux Bridge (yes, there is a bridge), also the crawfish capital of the world, and have lunch at the original Mulate's. It looks like an old dance hall, complete with wood floors and a bandstand. These floors have supported 5 generations of diners and dancers. French-speaking Cajuns, including the whole family, frequently come to Mulate's for the pleasure of eating, dancing, and having a good  time. In May, you can attend the Crawfish Festival in Breaux Bridge, one of the largest festivals in Cajun country. Enjoy Cajun food, music, dancers, exhibits, folklore, arts, crafts, and the Cajun people.

Nighttime in Cajun country brings many surprises. Brightly lit oil refineries appear like large cities with tall buildings, the air becomes filled with the indescribable sounds of the bayou, and the flash of little lights from fireflies.

Just a stone's throw from Breaux Bridge is Lafayette, the unofficial capital of Cajun country. A visit to the original Vermilionville (now Lafayette) Cajun and Creole Living History Museum and Folklife Village provides a quick historical introduction to the story of Acadian life, to the legend of Jean Lafitte, the pirate, and to the Acadian story that was the inspiration for Longfellow's "Evangeline".

Other Lafayette attractions essential in acquiring the essence of Southwest Louisiana are the Acadian Village, Cajun Country Store, Chretien Point Plantation, Lafayette Museum, Louisiana Museum of Military History, and St. John Cathedral, Cemetery, Museum, and Oak Tree. Near Vermilionville, we enjoyed dining at the much recommended Poor Boy's Riverside Inn. It was hard to find but worth the search to taste the wonderful flounder stuffed with crabmeat, fried alligator, gumbo, catfish, and their signature dessert, bread pudding. Started in 1931 by "Poor Boy" Hulo Landry, it is now run in the family tradition by his grandchildren. We stay in Lafayette for the night.

From Lafayette, take State Highway 90 to New Iberia, home of Shadows-on-the-Teche, where you can tour authentically restored antebellum homes, then tour Conrad Rice Mill, America's oldest.

The next stop is Avery Island, home of Tabasco. See how Tabasco is made, shop at the Tabasco store, look at fields of colorful Tabasco seed peppers being grown for next year's crops, and hear the history of the island and the McIlhenny family success story.

On down Highway 90 to Morgan City, home of Louisiana Shrimp and Petroleum Festival. This is the oldest chartered festival in Louisiana and is held every Labor Day weekend.

Back on Highway 90, stop at Houma. On the Bayou Teche, Houma sits among many waterways and bayous. At last, a place to take a real swamp and marsh tour. See alligators, rare birds, nutria, and other native wildlife. Charley drooled over the opportunities to fish, a favorite lifetime activity. Not this time, I finally persuaded. There were other important things to do before our plane left New Orleans. We had to eat at ABear's Cafe and hear some authentic local Cajun music. Dave's Cajun Cabin Cafe beckoned just down the road. So much to see and do, boy, was I getting the essence of Southwest Louisiana!

From Houma, we take 24 north to Highway 1 where we arrive in Thibodaux to visit Charley's kin and for me to experience beautifully restored Oak Alley sugar plantation, and numerous historical churches. Here I learned more history and absorbed more culture at the Wetland Acadian Cultural Center and Jean Lafitte National Historic Park and Preserve. My in-laws, Margaret and Julius Champagne took me on a voyage up the Bayou Lafourche. Sponsored by the Jean Lafitte

Painting by Julius Champagne

A "Cajun Country" Experience   **19**

National Historical Park, one of the six Jean Lafitte sites run by the Federal Park Service in Louisiana. I enjoyed the cruise and narrated history on the waterway that has been called the "World's Longest Street". We cruised to the magnificent Madewood Plantation where we lunched on crawfish etouffee and gumbo in the formal dining room. We delved into the heritage of this E.D. White plantation home with an unforgettable tour. It is currently a bed and breakfast (for information call 985-448-1375). Can you believe a restaurant called Bubba's? Well, it is a cozy family place on Bayou Lafourche, which runs through Thibodaux.

Nicholls State University billboard, in Thibodaux, announces a culinary school, started by Chef John Folse of Lafitte's Landing Restaurant fame. Chef Folse's accomplishments and credentials, including the American Culinary Federation's prestigious "National Chef of the Year" in 1990. His restaurants can be found in Hollywood, Moscow, Hong Kong, Japan, China, London, Paris, Rome, and Washington D.C. Back to Highway 10 we scurried. We must not miss our favorite treats in New Orleans before making like birds and flying back to California and home! In New Orleans, we stay at the Avenue Plaza on St. Charles.

Next morning after coffee in our room, we go to Felix's Restaurant for a catfish Poor Boy for me and oysters on the half-shell for Charley. How about 2 to 3 dozen? Back to St. Charles and Avenue Plaza for a brief rest. Supper is at Tujague's on Decatur in the French Quarter. The owner, Steve Latter, greets us and the head waiter begins to bring us the menu of the day. One of the oldest restaurants in New Orleans, it serves the same great Creole food it has always served. The courses keep coming, soup, salad, their famous brisket of beef, choice of roasted chicken, garnished heavily with potatoes, garlic, and parsley, or a selection of fresh fish or a steak. Yum! Ending with fantastic bread pudding with tart cranberry sauce. Off to hear the Louis Armstrong Society Band play a salute to Satchmo at the Bienville House Hotel in a Cabaret style theatre, "Hello Dolly!", great music. Back to Bourbon Street for our annual stroll, a hurricane and singing at Pat O'Brien's, then Preservation Hall, counting uniformed police, we feel safe, then, it's time for Cafe Du Monde's special treat of New Orleans, coffee and beignets. The end to a perfect day.

The next day, we breakfast on St. Charles at the Trolley Cafe on eggs, grits, biscuits, and gravy. Walk and inhale the fresh air. Back at the hotel, we read the Times Picayune. Charles reminisce experiences delivering it as a boy and his father working in its circulation department. We lunch across St. Charles at the Chef's Table. More catfish, I can't seem to get enough. This restaurant is owned by the Culinary Institute of New Orleans. It is operated to give students experience, the Chef instructor, Bob Koehl, tells us. A great experience for diner, also.

Back to the hotel for a nap. The last evening in Louisiana, gotta fly out the next morning. We confirm reservations for the dinner cruise aboard the Natchez. We go to the Riverwalk early so we can say "hi" to our friends at the Cajun Cooking School. You can have a delightful 2 hour lunch while watching the meal being cooked, with commentary about the history of Cajuns and their food. Last time we came away full of and with recipes for coffee latte, fried eggplant, Mardi Gras salad, jambalaya, and praline sauce over ice cream. We go to Jax Brewery (sorry, no more Jax's) and board the Natchez. We fill our plates at the buffet, more catfish, fried chicken, and too much for my overstuffed body. We sit as close to the stage as we can, as the Dukes of Dixieland are tuning up.

The next morning, we check out of our hotel, catch a cab, and go to the airport. As the plane ascends, I look out the window and think of all we are leaving behind. I look down at Lake Pontchartrain; it is so big, it looks like an ocean, then I remember, the catfish at Manshacks and drool for more catfish. Oh well, next year.

Refer to the Resource Guide for more information on many of the sights, restaurants, special events, and other things that may be of interest to you.

Ruth

THE CAJUNS: A HISTORY

Just what is a Cajun? Most Americans really don't know just what a Cajun is, so I am going to tell you.

It all starts in 1515 in the Duchy of Brittany on the coast of France. This was the year, through a political maneuver, Roman Catholic France acquired the Duchy. His Catholic Majesty, Francis I became the King of Brittany. Well, the good fishing folk of Brittany were mostly Protestants consisting of ancient Normans and Huguenots. There were sort of ambivalent about religion at best but they were reverent of life and lived it to the fullest. They ran into trouble right away with the French Inquisition and the strict Catholic-ruled state. Especially after fellow Frenchman, John Calvin, wrote in 1536 a treatise about Protestantism that made the Huguenot question a divisive French political and cultural problem.

In 1541, a group of Huguenots attempted, without success, to settle eastern Canada because French fisherman from Brittany and Normandy had been fishing the coast of Nova Scotia since the early 16th century. In 1600, Pierre de Tonnetuit, a Huguenot officer, was given the right of trade to the St. Lawrence basin by the King of France. His lieutenant, the Sieur de Monts, was given the right to colonize and engage in trade between the 40th and 46th parallels. This included Nova Scotia and the Acadian Peninsula. People from Brittany and Normandy then begin to emigrate to the Acadian Peninsula shores. The emigration didn't happen "en masse" until after 1624 when Cardinal Richelieu came to power in France. The Cardinal believed the people of Brittany and Normandy to be "workers for Satan". He excluded any Huguenot from owning any property in the New World and especially Nova Scotia. He also turned up the heat on the simple fishermen of Brittany and Normandy and the dreaded French Inquisition begin to take its toll.

The Huguenots, to escape this persecution, migrated by the thousands to Acadia. They built towns, cleared land for farms, built mills and churches. They built a virtual paradise. Fort Royal and Grand Pre' were the largest towns in the area. The towns were beautiful and self-governing, housing an independent fun-loving people.

During the last decade of the 17th century, Iberville and his brother, Bienville, explored what is now New Orleans and even went as far up the Mississippi to a place where a large red stick was planted on the river bank, hence the name "Baton Rouge".

New Orleans proper was settled in 1718 in the area of the present "French Quarter".

Things were not going well in the Old World, nor in the Acadian paradise for the people who only wanted to be left alone. In 1710 Francis Nickalson, Lieutenant Governor of Virginia with 3000 men attacked Acadian and captured it. Thus England took control of Nova Scotia. Bad times began in earnest for the happy people of Acadia.

The English government appointed Major Charles Lawrence as Lieutenant Governor of Nova Scotia in 1750. He did not trust the Huguenots, these people of Acadia; Lawrence tried to force them to give up all of their arms and swear an oath of submissiveness and allegiance to King George of England.

The free-thinking Acadians refused to do so. As Justin Wilson said, "They wouldn't swear allegiance to King George, they would only swear at him."

Lawrence then made plans to get rid of these trouble makers, and without compassion, he did.

In October of 1755, he directed twenty-four ships to the shores of Grand Pre'. The red coats marched into the homes and at bayonet point herded over 5000 Acadians, who had not hurt anyone, who only wanted to live their own lives, onto the ships and shipped them out. The English then burned Grand Pre' to the ground—over 700 homes! The Acadians refer to this as "Le Grand Derangement;" the English as "the Expulsion". Longfellow's epic poem, Evangeline, gives graphic detail of this tragedy.

Some of the ships landed in Maine, some in South Carolina, one went up Mobile Bay and a couple tried to go back to France. At least one ship sank with a loss of 700 souls. However, most of the ships had sense enough to make it to New Orleans, which still belonged to France.

New Orleans was already a city with a varied mixture of people of all races and cultures. The Acadians were homogeneous and close-knit—still are, for that matter. They just weren't content and didn't fit in with city life. They began looking for a place of their own to rebuild their homes— their paradise.

They settled up the banks of the Mississippi toward Baton Rouge (Red Stick) and down in the bayou country that nobody else wanted. They began building a new life.

People talked about these weirdoes from Acadia, Nova Scotia, with their strange language, habits and food. Over the years "Acadian" was shortened to "Cajun" and that's how the term "Cajun" evolved.

The story goes, when the Cajuns left Nova Scotia, the lobsters began to miss their Cajun friends a lot, and after a while the lobsters began a great migration in search of their friends. They went around the coast of Maine, down the eastern seaboard to the Mississippi. They went up the river and down the bayous until they found their lost friends. Since their diet had changed and they went from salt water to fresh, they shrank up and became crawfish. That's why Cajuns love crawfish so much.

Justin Wilson was the most famous Cajun story teller around. I have loved his stories since I attended Louisiana State University in the 50s, and heard him in person.

The first story I can remember him telling goes like this: One Sunday morning little Tejon and his daddy were reading the Sunday funny papers together. Tejon was lying on the floor by his daddy who sat in his big rocker. Tejon was reading Archie and was looking real hard at Veronica. He looked up at his daddy and timidly asked, "Daddy, what's a sweater girl, huh?" Well a question like that from his nine year old son took the old man by surprise, I'll tell you that. After a few minutes he cleared his throat and stuttered, "Oh, a sweater girl is a girl who works in a sweater factory. Where did you ever get a question like that?" Little Tejon carefully looked his daddy in the eyes and answered, "That's OK where I got a question like that, but where did you get an answer like that?"

Every parish (county) in "Cajun country" has its own "tellers of tales" and they're worth seeking out. Just ask anyone where they can be found.

Folks, these few pages just scratch the surface of Cajun history. There is so much to tell, so much to know about these truly fascinating people and their culture—a history full of tragedy, romance, pathos, and triumph. The book, "The Cajun" by William Faulkner Rushton, is one of my favorites and goes into great detail. It is listed in the bibliography.

All sports are very important in Louisiana. In fact our license plates carry the inscription "Sportsman's Paradise."

Sportsman's Paradise simply means Louisiana has the best all round, all year, hunting, fishing (salt and freshwater), golfing, boating, hiking, swamp touring and "gator" hunting in the U.S.A. Of course there are some sports that we can't mention here, but we're famous for them too, and they go on year round.

LOUISIANA—Come as you are. Leave different.
(Trademarked motto.) http//www.louisianatravel.com.

Charley

THE CAJUNS AND THEIR FOOD

People whose taste buds drool at the prospects of food full of flavors have the Huguenots and their 17th century persecutors, the French Inquisition, to thank. The freethinking freewheeling French Protestants, tired of politics, were granted land in Acadia by the King of France in 1604. Acadia included the present Canadian provinces of New Brunswick, Nova Scotia, Prince Edward Island and parts of Quebec and the state of Maine.

If your family name is, for example: Arceneaux, Aucoin, Babin, Boudreaux, Bourgeois, Cameaux, Champagne, Daigle, Dagas, Gaudet, Gautreaux, Hebert, Landry, Leblanc, Melancon, Naquin, Pitre, Prudhomme, Richard, Robichaux, Theriot, Thibodaux, or Trahan, you are most probably a descendant of the Acadians who were deported from their home land in 1755, victim of an eighteenth century war between France and England. When France ceded Canada to King George III these Acadian residents and land owners refused to sweat allegiance to the English King. The British put between 6,000 and 7,000 of them on ships one Sunday morning and deported them. This deportation was immortalized in Henry Longfellow's poem *Evangeline; A Tale of Acadie,* published in 1847. Most of those deported went to the English colonies of Massachusetts, Pennsylvania, South Carolina, Virginia and Georgia and some to the Islands of Guadeloupe and Martinique (now Santa Domingo) in the West Indies and some went back to France. Some say 25% of the Acadians died from epidemics, starvation and ships that were not seaworthy. Starting in probably 1756, but documented in 1765 many of these exiled found their way to the Louisiana Territory where the language, customs and religion were familiar. They bypassed New Orleans, which was too populated for their country stile of living and settled in the swamps of southwestern Louisiana. They settled along the Mississippi River in what is now St. James and Ascensions parishes, and along Bayou Lafourche and Bayou Teche, southwest of New Orleans. The Acadians engaged in farming, cattle raising and fishing. They loved this country and state for giving them a permanent home. They became know as Cajuns and perfected a regional diet known for it spice and flavor. Their descendants have made outstanding contributions to the political, educational, business and religious life of the state and Nation. The French language they speak has endured and is similar to that spoken in Normandy and western France.

"Ask 10 people what Cajun food is and nine of them are bound to say, 'hot'", writes Mark Binder in his article "Cajun Food Cool: Clarifying the

Cajun Conundrum," published in Food Distribution Magazine in August of 1998. He goes on to say, "The only problem is that Cajun food is not necessarily spicy."

Paul Prudhomme's cookbooks provide recipes for the home cook to prepare Cajun food. A misunderstanding in his first cookbook, Louisiana Kitchen, resulted in the myth that Cajun food was super hot. Paul Prudhomme is from Opelousas, Louisiana. The people in that area tend to use more red pepper in their cooking than they do in other areas. Paul Prudhomme explains, when he wrote the cookbook, Louisiana kitchen, he did not realize that the cayenne pepper available in most grocery stores across the United States was five to eight time hotter than the cayenne pepper grown in the Louisiana hot moist climate. Paul says. "Authentic Cajun Gumbo is awesome, it excites you to no end it's not just hot."

Manufacturers of foods began making spicy hot sauces and labeling them Cajun and putting them in stores. Restaurants and fast foods began adding peppers to everything from chicken to vegetable soup and calling it Cajun. They were just trying to imitate Cajun or their concept of Cajun. Store buyers have become aware and food manufacturer are not labeling products as Cajun unless they are authentic Cajun recipes.

Another misconception is that "blackening" is an old traditional way of cooking meats. Wrong! Paul Prudhomme "invented the process of blackening fish or meat by coating it with spices and searing it in a smoking hot cast-iron skillet." Twenty-five years ago redfish was abundant but had little flavor, this inspired Paul to create blackening to add flavor. He started serving it in his restaurant K-Paul's.

The next time you have the opportunity to eat or taste authentic Cajun gumbo, jambalaya, etouffee, andouille or boudin sausages, or anything authentically Cajun—go for it! You'll be glad you did.

Enola Prudhomme, owner of the Cajun Café in Carencro, Louisiana, says people will come back to Cajun food. She suggests starting with something simple that tastes good like jambalaya with sausage and chicken and a couple other kinds of meat. Enola is Paul's sister. Paul told me she prepares "unleaded food" because many of her recipes are low fat.

We use our eyes to evaluate the foods we eat. This experience illustrates this. I was cooking white Northern beans as part of the menu I was making for the weekly meal Charley and I cooked for a close friend who is a victim of strokes. I forgot the beans and they boiled dry, scorching one side of many. I had no time to prepare more so I rinsed them off, put them in another pan, added cut okra and seasoning and served them anyway. Curt, who is from Dallas, Texas, said, "Oh good, black-eyed peas," and ate a large second helping. I never said a word and kicked Charley under the table.

Laissez les bons temps rouler (let the good times roll).

Charley and Ruth

A LITTLE BIT OF HEAVEN ON EARTH

Do you know what it means
To miss New Orleans?

How do you begin to tell someone about this town? I have had a continuing love affair with New Orleans since the 1940s! Every time I revisit this city that "gave birth to the blues," I experience a rebirth of fascination and euphoria that no other place on this planet can produce. When you love this city—and you can't avoid this love affair—she'll haul off and love you right back.

"Nouvelle Orleans" was founded and named for the Duke of Orleans in 1718 by Bienville and for over twenty-six decades has been the "city that care forgot." In fact, New Orleans has many names and wears many faces: "America's Most Interesting City," "The Crescent City," "Creole Town," "Cotton Town," and some names that cannot be printed. This is the town of Jean Lafitte and Louis Armstrong (Satchmo), Al Hirt and Dorothy Lamour, Pete Fountain and Andrew Jackson, Jim Bowie and Tennessee Williams, Huey P. Long and Jelly Roll Morton, Dana Andrews and John J. Audubon, Harry Connick, Jr., beignets, streetcars, and more.

New Orleans is famous for many things, for example, Mardi Gras ("Carnival," as it is known locally), euphonious music, fantastic cuisine, Audubon Park, the Super Bowl, the Super Dome, the Mississippi River, paddlewheel boat rides, Preservation Hall, jazz funerals, the fabulous French Quarter, and it goes on and on.

Yes, the French Quarter—now we've said it. You'll fall in love with the incomparable atmosphere and laissez-faire attitude in the French Quarter, with all its Old World shops and buildings. You won't find anything like it anywhere else in the world.

New Orleans has so many wonderful sights and diversions to offer that it would take a book to tell about them, but the French Quarter, or "Vieux Carre" ("Old Square"), has to be *the* place in New Orleans. This is the section of town that was the original city. This is where New Orleans was born—and it is still the spiritual center or soul of the city.

A Mr. Bartlett, writing for a magazine called *Dixie* in 1776, thus described the city. "New Orleans fronts about 1,500 yards along the river and has a depth of 70 yards into 'La Cypriere' (the Great Cypress Swamp). The population is 1,803 whites, 96 free persons of color, 61 Indians and

1,227 slaves. This is undoubted not accurate, although it is the official count, as slaves are smuggled in, and there is a subculture of gamblers, thugs, exiles and drifters."

Touring the 80-some-odd blocks of the French Quarter is something one can do on foot—in fact, it's the only way to really enjoy it and absorb the particular flavor and aura of the area. Visit the Old Bank of the United States built in 1801 for the maternal grandfather of the French Impressionist painter, Edgar Degas. Don't miss Pirate's Alley, where Gen. Andrew Jackson and Jean and Pierre Lafitte conferred concerning the defense of New Orleans in 1814, the Presbytere that was built as a Capuchin monastery in 1788, and St. Louis Cathedral. This is the oldest cathedral in the United States and the third church on the site. The first house of worship was built about 1719 and was demolished by a hurricane in 1722. Its successor would endure until perishing in the cataclysmic fire of 1788. That fire destroyed most of the city. The present church was dedicated on Christmas Eve 1794, as a cathedral. In 1964, Pope Paul VI designated St Louis Cathedral as a minor basilica.

Walk out of the cathedral, turn right, and behold the Cabildo. During Spanish rule, this structure housed the governing council, or Cabildo, of the colony. The Cabildo, cathedral, and Presbytere face the green oasis called Jackson Square. This area was established in 1721 as a drill field and was first known as the Place d'Armes under the French and Plaza de Armas under the Spanish. Street artists abound on all four sides of the square. As a memento of your visit, purchase one of the artist portrayals of the area or get a portrait of yourself or loved one.

There are numerous other French Quarter attractions that should not be missed, such as the Old Ursulines Convent built in 1749, Lafitte's Blacksmith Shop, Café Du Monde, Tujague's Restaurant (Creole) started in 1856 to serve the dock workers, and Antoine's Restaurant (Creole), which is the oldest in the city. Visit KPaul's Louisiana Kitchen for great Cajun food. Most restaurants in New Orleans serve Creole food. Visit Jax Brewery. The building now houses shops and the New Orleans Cooking School, which offers a 2-hour cooking session for visitors and lunch as it is cooked. The old *Steamboat Natchez* ties up behind Jax to take you on a river cruise while you dine and listen and dance to live traditional jazz.

Near the Vieux Carre, during the Victorian era, was the "Storyville" district. The debauchery in the city had become the talk of the hemisphere, and the city fathers were moved to impose some restrictions. So alderman Sidney Story introduced an ordinance confining prostitutes, or "women notoriously abandoned to lewdness," to one specific area. It was soon called Storyville, much to Sidney's dismay. It covered an area of 38 blocks in and near the French Quarter. It was the biggest red-light district in the history of the United States.

This city has so much to see and enjoy, it will take several trips to discover and taste the essence of it all. Visit New Orleans and you too will know "what it means to miss New Orleans."

And then come on down to Cajun country!

Charley

CAJUN COUNTRY

Cajun Power read the bumper sticker in front of me as I followed a car off U.S. 90 onto the state highway for the last few miles to Thibodaux, Louisiana. I was traveling parallel to Bayou Lafourche, from which the parish (county) derived its name. A sign on my right advertised *CRAW-FISH FOR SALE,* while on my left a shrimp boat chugged slowly down the bayou toward the Gulf of Mexico.

The atmosphere, the aura, the mystical enchantment of the area permeated my senses. The lazy, meandering bayou was my "Magic River," the highway was my "Yellow Brick Road," and around the next bend I would discover the "Emerald City." The green and white sign proclaimed: *Welcome to Thibodaux, Louisiana, Queen City of Bayou Lafourche.*

I finally located my sister and brother-in-law's new home near Nicholls State University. It was on a circular street called Acadia Point. My sister and her husband honor their heritage by being informed about the how, why, when, and where of everything Cajun.

The original inhabitants of this part of the country were Bayougoula, Chitimacha, Ouacha, and Houmas Indians, who were members of the Colapissa Nation. They were known to have been in this area as early as 1686, and there is evidence they made alliances in 1699 with Iberville, the founder of Louisiana's first French settlement, who called them "bayou (river) people."

Bayou Lafourche branches off from the Mississippi River just below Baton Rouge and winds its way slowly and serenely down 30-odd miles to Thibodaux. The French named it "Lafourche," which means "the fork," because of the fork it made with the mighty Mississippi. It meanders its way through rich farmland, sugarcane fields, moss-laden cypress trees, and marshlands. The bayou reaches it outlet in the Gulf of Mexico some 80 miles below Thibodaux.

Bayou communities like Thibodaux were laid out with every family having a narrow frontage on the bayou. The land was measured in "arpents," not acres. An arpent is 192 linear feet. Each family or settler had an arpent fronting the bayou. Some of these parcels of land stretched back from the bayou as far as five or six miles.

The bayou frontage was necessary for transportation. The versatile "pirogue," a lightweight, canoe-type craft made out of a single cypress-tree trunk, was the primary vehicle. Many are still used to this day.

The "Cajuns" moved into Bayou Lafourche in large numbers, and eventually an unbroken chain of homes sprouted up along the entire length of the bayou, giving it the reputation of being "The Longest Main Street in the World."

I sampled a little bit of everything during my short stay. I visited beautiful, stately old plantation homes and enjoyed the cuisine. I learned about the local superstitions, legends, and customs.

There are many Acadian superstitions and legends. Close your eyes a moment and picture nightfall in Cajun country. You are sitting beside a bonfire. The bayou has a heavy mist rising from it that is cold and damp and smells like an open grave. The moss-laden cypress trees look like giant ghosts covered with silver, shimmering spider webs, and the strange sounds of the night convince you the bayou and swamp are alive! You involuntarily shiver, and you are not sure whether it's from the cold or that funny feeling of uncertainty that is forming in the pit of your stomach. An ol' Cajun sitting across from you clears his throat and startles you with his comment.

"It were on a night just like this one when me, I myself, first seen the 'haint'—and I tell you true, man, it weren't too far from this spot either."

A "haint" is the soul of a deceased child who was not baptized, condemned to wander endlessly in search of a place of rest. Many times it appears as a mysterious light, which attracts its victims into the swamps in a trancelike state and they are never heard from again.

I was instructed about the "Conjo"—a wicked spirit who casts spells with the aid of voodoo. To cast a spell he recites these words: *"L'appe vini, le grand Zombi. L'appe vini, pour tio gris-gris."*

I heard stories about the "Tataille," the "Couche Mal," and the "Loup Garou" (werewolf), all prominent in Acadian superstitions.

The Cajuns have many interesting legends. The legend of the crawfish intrigued me, as did the one about the Spanish moss.

When the Acadians were exiled from Nova Scotia, their friends, the lobsters, followed them all the way to Louisiana. Exhausted by their long journey, the lobsters wasted away but refused to leave their friends, the Acadians, and they became crawfish.

A young woman died of a broken heart during her fiance's long absence. The young Acadian returned to the oak tree where they had often met to speak of their love. He did not find her there—just a lock of her hair suspended from a branch of the tree. The lock, symbolic of fidelity and love, was transformed miraculously into Spanish moss. To this day, Spanish moss hangs from the trees of Acadia as a memorial to this great love.

When I left Thibodaux for a driving tour of the many beautiful old plantation homes in the area, it was nearly twelve hours before I returned. I visited 43 plantation homes. Some are still private residences and I could only view them from the road, but many were open to the public.

I visited homes with romantic names like Felicity, Evergreen,

Waguespack, Kismet, Zenon Trudeau, Helvetia, Tezcuco, Armitage, Magnolia, and Rosella. I visited beautiful Oak Alley, with its double row of live oaks, 14 on each side of the drive that stretches from the home to the road. The oaks, each 80 feet apart, are 200 years old.

Another beautiful home open to the public is San Fran/isco, built in 1849 by Valison Marmillion, who died before it was finished. He had used funds he was saving for a year of bad crops, and the home was originally named Son Saint Frusquin, literally translated as "I have lost my shirt."

After a few days of rest and enjoying the local cuisine and people, I felt sad that I had to leave. As the Queen City of Bayou Lafourche faded behind me, I remembered these hauntingly beautiful lines from Longfellow's *Evangeline.*

Meanwhile apart, in the twilight Gloom of a window's embrasure,
Sat the lovers, and whispered together, beholding the moon rise
Over the pallid sea, and the silvery mists of the meadows,
Silently one by one, in the infinite meadows of heaven,
Blossomed the lovely stars, the forget-me-nots of the angels.

Charley

THIS IS CRAZY CHARLEY

Charley learned to cook because he has a passion for eating. The kitchen has always been his favorite room in the house. When he was a boy, he followed the cook around the kitchen, watching, helping, tasting, and asking questions. His mother, Grandmother Oliver, Josephine (their household help), and the cooks of his cousins, aunts, and uncles, well, he stalked them all.

Charley's Grandmother Oliver helped him make good ole' southern fried corn bread when he was nine. From then on, he learned to prepare many of the foods he enjoyed. A BLT sandwich was a favorite with tomatoes available from the garden. He still loves to eat pot liquor left over from cooking collard, mustard, and turnip greens with crumbled corn bread. Charley bought a deep fryer with the first money he earned. It expedited the cooking of the piles of French fries he liked to eat after football practice.

Oscar, a 20th century descendant of the Acadians exiled from Acadia, Nova Scotia, lived in a 1 room shack at the edge of town. He remembered the Choctaw Indians, hunted squirrels, caught catfish, crawfish, and shrimp, once was treed for 9 days by wild pigs, and had a pet llama that could hit you in the eye at 20 paces with a wad of chewing tobacco.

Oscar was referred to as "that old crazy Cajun" by the town's people. Like many people who are different, he was viewed with distrust and fear by the "regular people". As an old man, he befriended Charley as a boy, entertaining him with tall tales of the swamp. The "crazy Cajun" helped young Charley perfect his fishing and hunting skills. Charley cleaned the fish, squirrels, quail, doves, rabbits, ducks, geese, and deer in the swamps near his home.

After supplying his family, he sold the rest to buy shotgun shells for his 12 gauge pump Winchester, .22 shells for his rifle, and fishing gear. Charley still enjoys fishing and hunting. His mother told me about all the game she cooked for the family but said she could never bring herself to eat any of it. She did love the catfish, bass, and perch cooked in the southern tradition. The story goes about the creative way Cajuns make a meal out of anything. In a Cajun zoo, each cage would include the animals common name, the scientific name, and a recipe.

Justin Wilson, whose mother was a Cajun, was among the first to let the secret out with his cookbooks and PBS Cajun cooking shows. Remember? A little wine for the pot and a little for him. Justin demonstrated the cooking of delicious mouthwatering Cajun recipes.

Paul Prudhomme extended the secret of Southern Louisiana cooking to the world. Paul's family are talented cooks. Paul Prudhomme didn't just follow home cooks around, he followed known chefs. He was inspired by a relative who became a cook in New Orleans after serving in the Navy as a cook during World War II. Impressed and challenged by the prospects of cooking for a living and making good money, young Paul made a fantasy commitment to become a professional cook. He wanted to cook something good and make it better than he had ever tasted it before. Paul has made his childhood vision come true to the delight of diners on the wonderful food he prepares at his restaurant, K-Paul's in New Orleans, and for special events around the world. His cookbooks are filled with recipes that are the best they can be.

Paul's sister, Enola (a family of 13 kids), started her Prudhomme's Cajun Cafe in Carencro, Louisiana, after her 5 children were grown. She serves delicious Cajun home-style food with many low-fat (Paul calls it unleaded) dishes on her menu. You can find these recipes in her book Enola Prudhomme's Low-Calorie Cajun Cooking.

Charley learned to cook to guarantee that quality and flavor are never missing from his meals. He still doesn't trust me to prepare a meal. He snoops around, questioning seasonings used, cooking time, and just watching, and most of all asking, "When is the food going to be ready? I am hungry!"

Cooking has always been a hobby, rather than a vocation, for Charley. As a young teen, he sold the New Orleans Time Picayune (named for the Spanish coin with the value of a penny over 200 years ago, the cost of a paper), worked as an egg candler and delivered fresh eggs to major restaurants in New Orleans. He watched the chefs prepare marvelous dishes and grew to love Creole and Cajun food even more. At home, his mother and Grandmother Oliver were respected for their Cajun and Creole dishes and Charley was eager to learn what they had to teach.

Charley joined the Navy soon after he graduated from high school. Inspired by Raiders of the Deep by Lowell Thomas (true stories of the daring exploits of German U-Boats in WWI), he volunteered for submarine duty. He spent 25 years in the Navy. He has cooked gumbo, jambalaya, and Cajun BBQ sauce all over the world for friends and colleagues.

Charley has combined his knowledge of cooking "Cajun" with his love of history. He is a teller of stories by the "Crazy Cajun," Oscar Robertson, and of the history of the Cajun people. He is an avid reader of history and historical novels.

Charley enjoys telling stories of different historical periods to students in history classes. He weaves Cajun stories into his cooking demonstrations at food shows and festivals. He perfected his storytelling skills in acting workshops held by Larry Minkin. (Larry played Captain Video and many excellent supporting roles in movies and TV.) Charley practiced his storytelling as a guest speaker at "men's clubs", Rotary, Sirs, and others in the San Francisco Bay area, often ending with a standing ovation.

Charley has put his family recipes in jars because his friends kept asking for jars of his wonderful Cajun sauces.

Charley wants you to enjoy making Cajun dishes in your kitchen. His gumbo base is Creole styled, his family's recipe used the tomatoes raised in their garden to make a tomato roux rather than the brown gravy roux often made for Cajun gumbo. Cajuns and Creoles have many common dishes, such as gumbo and jambalaya. Creoles, who are city dwellers, at times use a tomato based roux and more spice (Spanish influence). The Cajuns, who are country people, usually make a brown gravy roux.

Crazy Charley brand sauces will help you prepare Cajun and Creole meals that are easy, quick, and delicious. Just follow the simple recipes presented in this book.

Use recipes from this book to plan a fais-do-do (fay-doe-doe). A fais-do-do, or gathering, is an important part of life for the Cajun folk of South Louisiana. They are happy, friendly, fun loving, and family oriented. You can host a fais-do-do for your friends, family, or community.

Cook Cajun food, listen to Cajun music, attend a Cajun festival near your home, take a vacation to Cajun country—you'll be glad you did, I guarantee!

Ruth

TWO OF MY FAVORITE CAJUNS

I care about people from South Louisiana, but there are two men who have made a great impression on my life. These men have done much to spread the "Cajun" image and cuisine around the world. I hold these two in the highest esteem.

PAUL PRUDHOMME, Cajun chef extraordinare. I first met Paul some years ago when he was a chef at the famous Commanders Palace in the Garden District of New Orleans.

Paul is a gentle man, a gentle giant, if you will. Even though he has been afforded much acclaim throughout the world, he remains unpretentious. He never strays too far from his beginnings as the youngest of thirteen children raised on a farm near Opelousas. He can tell you even now how good his momma could cook and how emotional the family was about their food.

Paul became a professional cook, a chef, fulfilling a childhood dream.

Then in the mid-1980s, Paul and his talented late wife, K, opened K-Paul's Louisiana Kitchen in New Orleans. It is one of the "must" restaurants in the city, the best of the best!

Thanks Paul for being you and as your autograph always proclaims, "Good Cooking! Good Eating! Good Loving."

JUSTIN WILSON, purveyor of Cajun humor and cuisine. I first heard of Mr. Wilson back in the 1950s while attending LSU in Baton Rouge. He was a prodigious spinner of Cajun humor. His tales, as he is himself, are known the world over. We all have seen him cook on TV and, I hope, purchased one or more of his books.

I believe he became a chef because he is a man who lived to eat and to cook too, you hear!

I realize some folk in the Acadian area believe Justin's stories make the Cajun people seem ridiculous and crude. Justin was out there pitching "Cajun" before anyone else. People who can't laugh at themselves have no real sense of humor and I know Cajuns have a wonderful capacity for humor.

Thank you, Justin, for the joy and laughter you brought to all of us. You were the best, I guarantee! We miss you, bro!

Charley

CAJUN SAUCE (ALL-PURPOSE AND BBQ) AND RECIPES

CRAZY CHARLEY CAJUN BAR-B-QUE SAUCE

16-oz. bottles, all natural, no MSG or cholesterol. No added fat or oil and no added salt. Only 29 calories an ounce. This fine product has a brewed-coffee base and the recipe is over 100 years old. It is simply the best BBQ sauce in the world...I guarantee!

COOKING WITH CAJUN SAUCES
(All-purpose and BBQ)

Barbeque: This term denoting at first an elevated platform or framework used for outdoor cooking. The word comes from barbacoa of Caribbean Haitian origin and from American Spanish baracoa. Webster tells us that the word barbecue means, "1. to roast or broil over an open fire, 2. a social gathering, especially in the open air at which barbecued food is eaten, 3. a party, picnic, or restaurant featuring this, 4. a highly seasoned sauce of vinegar, spices, etc." Currently, the word barbecue is in transition with "grill", meaning the method of cooking and the word barbecue designating the highly seasoned flavor.

The Reader's Digest, *Down Home Cooking* (1994), tells us, "Barbecue means something different everywhere you go," says Jim Quessenberry, International Barbecue Champion from Cherry Valley, Arkansas. "In Kansas City, barbeque is done over charcoal and slathered with a sauce that's heavy on tomatoes and liquid smoke. They often begin by rubbing meats and poultry with a dry spice rub before placing them on the grill, then mop on the sauce only during the last half hour."

"In the Great Lake States, folks cook over fires seasoned with chips of fruitwood and baste with sauces containing more sweetness than spice."

"Throughout California and Washington, the locals often barbecue with Oriental sweet and sour sauces, which may include such Polynesian ingredients as pineapple."

"In the back country in the Carolinas, the sauces are mostly spicy vinegar concoctions—no tomato at all. Day-long barbecue feasts called pig pickin's are common there."

"On the plains and ranches of Texas, barbecues are often community affairs. The barbecue pits are fired up with a mixture of charcoal and sticks of pecan, hickory, or oak. Beef briskets and ribs are usually on the menu and they're generously mopped with thick sauce that's described as 'the spicier, the better!'"

"In New England, where the winters are cold, barbecue commonly refers to any food that is smothered with a smoky sauce, then cooked in the oven."

"All around the country, barbecue times frequently means 'Y'all come' times, with lots of good food and plenty of fun."

Broiling and grilling outdoors over an open fire of burning charcoal, fruit woods, or propane fired bricks has been a favorite national pastime for decades. You can spend thousands of dollars on barbecue equipment or you can cook without any, as campers and woodsmen do. You can use all you know about indoor broiling. You just need to remember the source of heat is below the food you are cooking where you have less heat control. Arrange your coals so half the grill has a hot fire and the other half a slow fire for cooking after searing. You can wrap food in foil and bury it in the coals (as in a campfire), potatoes, large hunks of meat, etc.

People are so mobile that you can find all styles of barbecuing almost anywhere. We all agree, any way you do it, it's great.

SELECTING A BARBECUE SAUCE

There are numerous barbecue sauces on the market and many ideas of how barbecue sauce should taste. How does one select the right barbecue sauce? Many sauces have smoke flavor added to take the place of the smoke taste provided when foods are cooked over woods such as hickory, mesquite, oak, or pecan. Sauces that are made for use over foods cooked on wood fires are usually strong with spicy vinegars and the wood adds the smoke flavor. Barbecue sauces come with different levels of heat, some very mild, others XXXX spicy hot, and every degree between. You may want to consider nutritional factors, such as fat, salt, sugar content, and natural ingredients.

More home cooks are using barbecue sauces year round, because their families enjoy the flavor. Barbecuing chicken, ribs, roasts, lamb, pork, game, and vegetables in your kitchen oven makes a great meal for a cold winter evening. Kitchen ovens are great to broil or roast meats and vegetables. Slow oven cooking adds warmth and wonderful aromas to your home.

Barbecue sauce is a versatile sauce. Barbecue sauces can be used as a flavoring in many recipes. The recipes in this book use *Crazy Charley* brand Cajun BBQ sauce as a seasoning and flavor enhancer. It has a wonderful complex taste that complements many different foods. The recipes are quick and easy to prepare.

Crazy Charley's Cajun sauce comes in 3 heats, original, hot, and Cajun hot. It has won many national and regional competitions because of "balance of heat and flavor, great smoke flavor, robust! deep and rich..."

Our Cajun sauce (all-purpose and BBQ) comes from Thibodaux, Louisiana. The recipe has been traced back 120 years. It has been passed down for generations and everyone who tastes "The Sauce" falls in love with it and I guarantee you will, too!"

Crazy Charley brand Cajun sauce has a coffee base and the heat source is Tabasco brand pepper sauce. The more Tabasco used, the hotter it is; pepper seeds are added to the Cajun hot, our hottest. (Read the section on Piquante Salsa to learn more about peppers.) Cajun sauce has all natural ingredients, low sodium, no fat, no MSG or preservatives, and only 25 calories per 2 tablespoons serving.

Many of the following recipes ask you to add the Cajun sauce before cooking. The wonderful flavor of the sauce gets tastier the longer it simmers, as it enhances the flavor of the rest of the ingredients.

As a home cook, you will find new ways to use this sauce in your recipes. Credit is given to customers who have shared recipes.

SUGGESTED USES FOR CAJUN SAUCES

As a barbecue sauce.
To season your Bloody Mary.
A dip for French bread and tortilla chips.
A seasoning for tomato based soups, stews, and sauces, i.e., spaghetti sauce.
Hot fondue for dipping shrimp, cubes of ham, and other precooked meats.
As a glaze for your favorite meat loaf.
As a glaze over ham. As a spread for meat sandwiches, i.e., turkey, baloney, and steak.
Add fresh grated ginger, garlic, or honey to vary the flavor as a barbecue sauce.
Dilute with equal parts of water, heat, and use as a marinade sauce; add ginger or garlic.

Serve as a hot dip with sausages and meatballs heated in the sauce; serve with toothpicks.

As a spicy catsup for potatoes, eggs, or ?

Add a teaspoon to oysters on the half shell before grilling.

Baste with or brush on 10 inch skewers of assorted meats and vegetables before grilling.

Brush on swordfish, red snapper, catfish, and tuna steaks and grill, broil, or bake for 8 to 12 minutes, until opaque in the center.

Add honey, curry, or mustard to vary flavor of Cajun sauces for chicken, ribs, burgers, and lamb.

Add 2 to 4 tablespoons to tomato based spaghetti sauce, soups, and stews; yum!

Use as a dip with your favorite chips.

BBQ CREAM CHEESE DIP

1 c. Charley's Cajun sauce (hot or mild)
12 oz. soft cream cheese (regular, light, or nonfat)

Combine the 2 ingredients in a bowl and beat with a whisk until smooth; use a blender or food processor. Turn out into serving dish and garnish with fresh mint or parsley. Serve with cocktail crackers, potato chips, vegetables, (cut into 2 inch sticks), or your favorite things to dip. Finger licking good!

Lagniappe: Pour a cup of Crazy Charley's piquante/salsa over this BBQ Cream Cheese Dip for a festive visual and taste appeal.

QUICK DIP

Pour a cup of Crazy Charley Cajun sauce over an 8-ounce block of softened cream cheese. Surround with assorted crackers and chips and a small knife for serving.

GRILLING HAS MYSTICAL POWER

Charley remembers families grilling, barbecuing, or cooking out in their backyards on outdoor grills made of bricks. What a way to party. That wonderful aroma drew family and friends like some mystical power.

Today, excellent portable grills are available and many kitchens have built in grills. Meats are often rubbed with a dry seasoning or marinated before grilling or barbecue sauce is smeared on the meat several times as it cooks. Many kinds of hardwoods are used to add flavor to the meat with marinade and barbecue sauce provided at the table. The choice is yours.

So, when someone says, "Let's eat out," plan a barbecue in your backyard.

TIPS FOR GRILLING OR BARBECUING

Make sure the grill rack is clean, oil the grill, and test for heat before putting food on it. Use a wire brush for cleaning and basting brush to apply oil. Do not use an oil spray on the grill rack.

Marinate meats, poultry, and seafood in the refrigerator for food safety. Protect cooked food; discard used marinade or boil it before using it as a basting sauce.

Brush barbecue sauce on cooked side of grilled foods, after it has been seared on the hot grill.

Blanch vegetables before grilling; baste with oil, then place on grill to prevent sticking. Baste with sauces on cooked sides.

To cut cooking time, parboil chicken 5 to 7 minutes before grilling. Baste with oil before placing on hot grill and baste with sauces. Best to cook chicken over medium heat; cover with lid of grill or fashion a lid with aluminum foil to hold heat in. Uncover to brown. This prevents burning and holds in heat and flavor. Be sure chicken is well done to kill salmonella.

Hardwoods, such as hickory, apple, pecan, walnut, etc. provide a hot clean fire. Soft woods do not produce coals. Oak and mesquite provide a stronger smoke taste.

Avoid the smell and taste of lighter fluids. Buy or make a charcoal lighter can.

How long you grill meats depends on 3 factors. 1. The thickness of the meat. 2. Temperature of the fire. 3. Distance from the fire to the meat. Meat 1 inch thick should be cooked 8 to 15 minutes 6 inches directly over the fire; 8 minutes for rare to 15 minutes for well done. Meat 2 inches thick, grill 20 to 30 minutes over medium fire. To cook 3 to 4 inch thick roasts, whole chickens, or leg of lamb, place over indirect heat; move coals to the side of the grill so the fire is not directly under the meat. Cover the barbecue (open vents) and cook, without turning, for 40 to 50 minutes, until brown and as done as you desire.

Grill is hot when you can hold your hand at grill level to the count of 2000, 3000. Grill is medium if you can hold your hand at grill level to the count of 4000, 5000.

Meat is rare when it is red inside and pale pink on the outside. It is medium when it is pink in the center and brown on the outside.

Keep your menu simple enough that you have time to enjoy the aroma of what's cooking and able to talk with friends and family.

CAJUN DOGS A LA KIM

8 Louisiana hot links
1 large onion, chopped
1 pkg. hot dog buns or steak rolls
Crazy Charley Cajun sauce of choice

Grill or steam hot links. Serve on bun with Cajun sauce and chopped onions. *Wow!* Serve with a salad and chips. Serves 6 to 8.

BARBEQUED RIBS

3 to 4 lb. any kind of ribs
1 c. Crazy Charley Cajun sauce of choice
1 tsp. salt

Cut meaty ribs (spareribs, beef, or ?) into servings. Place in roasting pan. Salt and pour Cajun sauce over meat. Cover and bake in at 350-degree oven for $1^1/_2$ hours. Baste and turn twice. Uncover the last 15 minutes. Serve with favorite salads and breads. Serves 4 to 6.

Lagniappe: Sprinkle 1 tablespoon grated ginger or garlic over ribs, then add sauce.

BARBECUED BEEF BRISKET

1 (3 to 4 lb.) boneless brisket of beef
1 large sliced onion
3 minced garlic cloves
1 c. Crazy Charley Cajun sauce
1 tsp. salt

Place meat, trimmed fat side up, on rack in baking pan (or wrap in foil for outdoor grill). Sprinkle salt over meat and place garlic and onion slices on top of brisket. Bake 50 minutes at 350 degrees. Remove from oven and pour Crazy Charley sauce over meat; cover. Bake for $1^1/_2$ hours more at 325 degrees. Remove from oven and let stand for 10 minutes, still covered. Place meat on platter or cutting board and slice across grain. Skim off fat from juice and ladle sauce over each serving. Serve with horseradish, roasted potatoes, vegetable, salad, and bread of choice. Serves 6 to 8.

Surprise your diners; serve this as an extra course, just before the main entree.

LOUISIANA LIMA BEANS AND HAM HOCKS SUPREME

1 lb. dried lima beans or white beans
1 large onion, cut into sixths
4 small ham hocks
2 bay leaves
3 cloves garlic, quartered
1 tsp. salt
1 c. Crazy Charley Cajun sauce of choice (original, hot, or Cajun hot)

Wash beans and place in large pot or Dutch oven; cover with cold water. Bring beans to a boil; simmer for 5 minutes. Let stand for 10 minutes, then drain water. Rinse and cover with cold water 3 inches above beans. This eliminates 80% to 90% of gas producing contents. Add onion, garlic, ham hocks, bay leaves, and salt. Cover and bring to a boil; reduce heat. Simmer for $1^1/_2$ hours or until just tender. Add Cajun sauce; simmer until beans are tender. Serve with cole slaw and corn bread. Serves 4.

Lagniappe: Top with piquante to garnish servings at the table.

VEGETABLE PASTA SAUCE

1 c. chopped onions
$^1/_2$ c. diced bell pepper
2 ribs diced celery
3 cloves minced garlic
1 c. diced zucchini
2 Tbsp. olive oil
1 c. sliced mushrooms
1 lb. pasta of choice

1 c. tomato sauce
2 c. stewed tomatoes
1 c. water
1 tsp. salt
2 tsp. oregano
1 tsp. Cajun powder

Saute vegetables in olive oil until tender in a medium size deep skillet. Add remaining ingredients and simmer for 30 minutes. Cook pasta. Serve sauce over pasta; sprinkle with your favorite grated cheese. Serve with a green salad and sweet French bread. Serves 6 as a main dish.

Lagniappe: Use this vegetable sauce as a side dish with meats, as you would ratatouille or fruit chutney. Add chopped eggplant when available. For a great ragout, add stew meat and 1 teaspoon Cajun powder. Use crab or shellfish boil in the water you boil your paste in to give the paste a great flavor.

BBQ BEANS (Quick and easy)

2 (15 oz.) cans pork and beans, drained
1 c. Crazy Charley Cajun sauce
$^1/_2$ lb. smoked sausage, cut bite-size and sautéed until browned

In medium heavy saucepan, place drained beans, Cajun sauce, and sautéed sausage; bring to a boil. Simmer for 5 minutes. Let stand for 10 minutes. Serve with BBQ meats, green salad, and sweet French bread. Serves 6.

Lagniappe: Double the recipe; place in crock-pot to take to potlucks, picnics, or barbecues.

RAISIN GLAZE FOR HAM OR TURKEY

1 c. Cajun sauce
1 c. crushed pineapple
$^1/_2$ c. raisins
$^1/_4$ c. brown sugar

Place all ingredients in heavy saucepan. Simmer for 10 minutes, stirring frequently. Pour over ham, turkey, or ? When meat is halfway baked. Return glazed meat to the oven; bake until done.

QUICK BEEF BARBECUE BAKE

1 lb. ground beef
$^1/_2$ c. diced onion
1 c. Cajun sauce
2 c. shredded cheese (Jack, Cheddar, or ?)
1 c. biscuit mix
1 c. milk
2 eggs

Heat oven to 400 degrees. Sauté beef and onions in skillet until brown; drain. Add Cajun sauce; spoon into a 13x9 inch-baking dish. Sprinkle $1^1/_2$ cups cheese on top. Beat baking mix, milk, and eggs well; pour over beef mixture. Top with $^1/_2$-cup cheese. Bake 25 minutes, until browned. Serves 8.

BARBECUED GINGER CHICKEN

You will need a $2^1/_2$ to $3^1/_2$ pound fryer, cut up and skinned.
Mix together:

1 c. Cajun sauce
$^1/_4$ c. honey
1 tsp. ground ginger

Rub chicken pieces with salt and pepper or use Cajun powder. Place in a 9x13 inch-baking dish; pour on sauce. Bake at 350 degrees for 1 hour. Cook, uncovered, to brown. Serve with baked yams and apple salad. Serves 3 to 4.

RED BEANS AND RICE

1 lb. red beans (or pinto beans)
1 large onion, cut into eighths
3 ribs celery, chopped
1 tsp. salt

1 Tbsp. Cajun powder
1 lb. smoked sausage, cut into 6 pieces
1 c. Charley's Cajun sauce
5 c. steamed rice (2 c. uncooked)

Rinse beans; cover with cold water and bring to a boil. Boil 5 minutes; drain and rinse again. Cover with 3 quarts of cold water or good chicken, beef, or vegetable stock and bring to a boil. Cover; simmer for 1 hour. Add onion, celery, Cajun powder, and sausage.* Simmer on low until tender; stir occasionally. Add more liquid as needed to prevent scorching. Remove lid and add Cajun sauce; simmer for 10 minutes. Just before beans are tender, steam your choice of brown or white rice. Serve with French bread and cole slaw. Serves 6 to 8.

*Lagniappe: Add diced green bell peppers and garlic with vegetables. Add fresh chopped green onions and parsley for garnish.

OUTDOOR BBQ OR GRILLING

8 oz. chicken, pork, ribs, steak, or ?? hot links sausages, hamburger (*per person*)
Salt and pepper
Crazy Charley's Cajun sauce of choice (original, hot, or Cajun hot)

Use a medium hot bed of coals or propane fire. If you can't count to 3000 by 1000's with your hand near meat level over the grill fire, it's too hot for medium hot cooking. Ouch, don't burn your hand.

BBQ as you normally do. Salt and pepper meat or rub with Cajun powder. Baste with Cajun sauce periodically as you turn the meat. BBQ 1 inch slices of vegetables as a side dish; brush with Cajun sauce on each side. Turn vegetables once during grilling. (Use zucchini, onion, yams, sweet potatoes, bell peppers, eggplant, apples, carrots, or ?.) Serve with BBQ beans and French bread.

Lagniappe: To Crazy Charley's Cajun sauce, add fresh grated ginger, garlic, honey, horseradish, or ? to vary BBQ taste.

CRAZY CHARLEY'S MEAT LOAF

1 lb. ground turkey
$^1/_2$ lb. lean ground beef
2 Tbsp. sage
1 egg, beaten
1 tsp. salt and pepper
$^1/_2$ c. onion, finely chopped
$^1/_2$ c. bell pepper, finely chopped
$^1/_2$ c. celery, finely chopped
$1^1/_2$ c. dried breadcrumbs
$^1/_2$ c. Cajun sauce of choice

Mix ground meats, sage, egg, salt, pepper, and vegetables until well blended. Add breadcrumbs and 1 cup Cajun sauce and fold until mixed. (Wash hands; mix the ingredients with your fingers. Feels good as bare feet in the sand.) Shape into a ball and pack into a loaf pan. Pour remaining Cajun sauce over the top. Bake in 350-degree oven for $1^1/_4$ hours or until done. Let set for 10 minutes before removing from pan. Serve with roasted potatoes or rice, green beans, fresh sliced tomatoes, and bell peppers.

SHREDDED BARBECUED BEEF

3 to 4 lb. lean beef roast
$^1/_4$ c. flour
Salt and pepper (or use 1 tsp. Cajun powder)
3 Tbsp. olive oil
2 c. Crazy Charley Cajun sauce of choice (original, hot, or Cajun hot—ouch!)
8 buns or sandwich rolls

Trim roast of fat; dredge in seasoned flour. Heat olive oil in a 4 to 6 quart pressure cooker or use a heavy pot roast pan. Brown meat it oil; add vegetables and brown. Add water and 1 cup of Cajun sauce; cover and pressure for 30 minutes or simmer as for pot roast $2^1/_2$ hours or until tender. Let stand until cooled before removing. Place meat on cutting board; shred by cutting meat into thin slices or pull apart with a fork. Return meat to pot. Add remaining Cajun sauce and bring to a boil. Simmer for 10 minutes. Serve on buns or large rolls with chips, coleslaw, potato salad, or coleslaw and chips. Serves 8.

Delicious, *I guarantee!*

PO BOY

A very popular sandwich in New Orleans and south Louisiana, always made with French bread. Paul Prudhomme tells us, "The first Po Boy was created during the Depression years at a New Orleans bar located along the streetcar tracks near the Mississippi river front. Many longshoremen bought their lunch there, and the owner created a long sandwich big enough to fill a hungry working man, and cheap enough for the poor boys in the depressed waterfront."

These classic sandwiches can be filled with fried fish, shrimp, crawfish, crab, oysters, Andouille sausage, meatballs, roast beef, ground beef, or ?. They are "dressed" with traditional fixings, such as sliced tomatoes, pickles, mayonnaise, and lettuce. The soft inner part of the bread is sometimes pinched out and replaced with fried seafood and flavored mayonnaise or other fillings. This is called a "loaf." Soft sweet French bread is used for both the "loaf" and "Po Boy."

GROUND BEEF LOAF

1 lb. lean ground beef
$^1/_2$ c. diced onion
$^1/_2$ c. diced bell peppers
Salt and pepper (or Cajun powder)
$^1/_2$ to 1 c. Charley's Cajun sauce
4 to 6 sweet French rolls, split

Brown beef, diced onions, peppers, and seasoning to taste. Add Crazy Charley's Cajun sauce. Cover and simmer 15 minutes. Pinch out some of the soft insides of French rolls; spoon in beef. Serve with chips. Serves 4 to 6.

CAJUN CRANBERRY MEATBALLS

Mix equal parts of your favorite Crazy Charley brand BBQ Cajun sauce with whole canned cranberries in an electric skillet; add meat balls and heat until hot. Serve with festive toothpicks or on a buffet. Try this one with smoked sausages.

PO BOY

Fry catfish or seafood of choice, Andouille or other good smoked sausage, chicken breasts, or use leftover meats and gravy, meatballs in sauce on French bread. Makes a great sandwich. Dredge seafood in a fish fry before deep-frying or sautéing in a little olive oil. (Fish fry recipe is in the Fried Catfish recipe, Cajun Powder chapter.) Dress your Po Boy as you would any other sandwich. I like lettuce, tomatoes, tartar sauce on fish, and pickles. Meats with gravy and sauces need nothing else. Serve with coleslaw and French fries.

> If you introduce a tomato product to dry beans before they
> have cooked long enough to be tender, they may not get
> soft at all. The acidity of the tomatoes keeps them hard.

A FAIS DO DO

An important part of the Cajun life was the "Fais Do Do." If you had a large home or barn, you would more than likely host a Fais Do Do for your extended family or community. Fais Do Do in Cajun (French) means "Baby go to sleep." After arriving at the party, the mothers would feed the little ones and put them in a room on pallets and admonish them to go to sleep, baby (Fais Do Do). Then the grownups would gather together, put on a pot of gumbo or jambalaya, ice down some beer, kick off their shoes and have a party, where they would dance, sing, eat, drink and have fun.

REAL MEN

Barbecuing is the only type of cooking a real man will do. When a man says, "Hey, let's have a barbecue tonight. I'll cook and you can relax!", this is what happens . . .

1. The man goes out to the patio, grabs a beer, and begins to prepare the grill.
2. The woman goes to the store and buys all vegetables, meat, paper plates, and so on
3. The woman washes and chops the vegetables, fixes the salad, and prepares the vegetables and side dishes and dessert.
4. The man sits down with another beer, lights the grill, and observes it for a while to make sure it's working.
5. The woman prepares the meat for cooking, places it on a tray along with the necessary cooking utensils, and takes it to the man, who is lounging beside the grill, making sure it stays lit.
6. The man ceremoniously places the meat on the grill.

7. The woman goes inside to get the plates ready and check the vegetables.

8. The man double-checks the beer cooler and has another one. The woman comes back out to remind the man that the meat is burning.

9. The man takes the meat off the grill and hands it to the woman.

10. The woman prepares the plates and brings them to the table.

11. After eating, the woman clears the tables, disposes of the trash and does the dishes.

12. The man grabs a beer and goes inside to watch the game.

13. The woman goes back outside and turns off the grill.

14. The man asks the woman how she enjoyed her night off. Upon seeing her annoyed reaction, he concludes that there's just no pleasing some women!

WHAT DID YOU WIN LAST TIME?

A very drunk Cajun goes into a bar and orders a drink. The bartender serves him and asks him if he would like to try the bar game of darts. Three in the bulls-eye and you win a prize. Only one dollar for three darts.

The Cajun agrees and throws the first dart. A bulls-eye!! He downs another drink, takes aim on wobbly feet, lets go...another bulls-eye!!! Two more quick drinks go down. Barely able to stand he lets go of the last dart. Three bulls-eyes!!!

All are astounded. No one has ever won before. The bartender searches for a prize . . . grabs a turtle from the bar's terrarium and presents it to the Cajun as his prize.

Three weeks pass . . . the Cajun returns and orders more drinks, then announces he would like to try the dart game again. To the total amazement of all the local drunks, he scores three more bulls-eyes and demands his prize.

The bartender, being sort of drunk himself, and a bit short on memory, doesn't remember what he gave before, so he asks the Cajun, "Say, what did you win the last time?"

And the Cajun responds, "A catfish sandwich on a hard roll."

CAJUNS PLAY GOLF

A couple of oil rich Cajuns decided to play one of those resort golf courses in Palm Springs. Upon arrival, the two Cajuns were told they couldn't play because there were no caddies available. "Well heck," one said, "we don't care, we' take a Buick."

BOUDREAUX AND THIBODEAUX BUY SUITS AND SHIRTS

Boudreaux and Thibodeaux are from Louisiana visiting a relative at the Huntsville, Texas prison. Walking along Sam Houston Street, they see a sign which reads: Suits $5.00 each, shirts $2.00 each, trousers $2.50 per pair.

Boudreaux says to his pal, "Hey, Thib, LOOK! We could buy a whole lot of those, and when we get back to Lafayette, we could make a fortune. Now when we go into the shop, you be quiet, okay? Just let me do all the talking 'cause if they hear our Cajun accent they might not serve us. I'll speak in my best Texas drawl."

They go in and Boudreaux orders 50 suits at 5.00 each, 100 shirts at 2.00 each and 50 pairs of trousers at 2.50 each.

The owner of the shop says, "You're from Louisiana, aren't you?"

"Oh . . . yes," says a surprised Boudreaux. "How come you know dat?" The owner says, "Cause this is a dry-cleaners!"

BOUDREAUX GOES FISH'N

Boudreaux been fish'n down by de bayou all day an he done run outa worms. He be bout reddy to leave when he seed a snake wit a toad frog in hits mout. He knowed that them big bass fish like toad frogs so he decided to steal dat froggie. That snake, hit be a cottn mouthed water moccasin so he had to bee real careful or he'd get bit.

He snuck up behind the snake and grabbed his roun the haid. That ole snake din't lik dat one bit. He squirmed an wrapped hisself roun Boudreaux's arm try'n to get himself free, but Boudreaux, him, had a real good grip on his haid, yeh.

Well, Boudreaux pried hit's mout open and got de frog and puts it in his bait can. Now, Boudreaux knows that he cain't let go dat snake or hit's gonna bite him good, but he had him a plan.

He reached into the back pocket of his bib overhauls and pulls out a pint o' moonshine likker. He pours a couple of draps inta the snake's mout.

Well, that snake's eyeballs roll back in hits haid and hits body go limp. Wit dat Boudreaux toss's dat snake inta the bayou den he goes back to fishin.

A while later Boudreaux dun feel sumpin tappin on his barefoot toe. He slowly look down and dare dat water mocassin was wit two toad frogs in his mout.

CAJUN MARKETING

A Cajun named Jean Paul moved to Texas and bought a donkey from an old farmer for $100. The farmer agreed to deliver the donkey the next day.

The next day, the farmer drove up and said, "Sorry, but I have some bad news. The donkey died."

"Well den, just give me mah money back."

"I can't do dat. I went out and spent it already."

"Ok, then. Just unload da donkey."

"What ya gonna do with him?" asked the farmer.

"I'm gonna raffle eem off."

"You can't raffle off a dead donkey?"

"Sure, I can. Watch me I jest won tell anybody he dead," said the Cajun.

A month later the farmer met up with the Cajun and asked, "What happened with that there dead donkey?"

"Ah raffle eem off. I sold 500 tickets at two dollars a piece and made ah profit of $998."

"Didn't any complain?"

"Jus da guy who won . . . so I give eem his two dollar back."

The moral of this story . . . marketing is everything!

MARINADE AND RECIPES

CRAZY CHARLEY MARINADE

16-oz. bottles of all-natural meat marinade that is just as good used as a stir-fry or fajita sauce. This wonderful product is winning acclaim and prizes all over the country and in England and Australia. It's the premier marinade in the world!

MARINADE

Marinade: According to Webster, a marinade is a "liquid preparation in which meat or fish is soaked to enrich its flavor." To *marinate* is "to soak in a marinade." Marinating onion, cucumber, watermelon rinds, and carrots or a mixture of these vegetables in vinegars, oils, herbs, and spices has been a style of preparing these foods for eating pleasure. Marinating foods is a part of many different cultures and is called by different names, pickled, chutney, relish, etc.

Marinating of meats has become more popular in the 1990s. A recent study showed that marinated chicken had less or no salmonella after it was cooked, while chicken cooked without marinade had signs of the bacilli. Most marinades have vinegar, wines, or soy sauce low in pH factors and prevent bacteria from growing. Marinating enhances the flavor of meats and many have papain or other enzyme to tenderize tough cuts of meat. Marinades are also used for stir-frying meats and vegetables.

TIPS FOR MARINATING

Use Tupperware or plastic Ziploc bags to marinate meats. They can be easily stored in the refrigerator and should be turned often.

Add fresh grated ginger, garlic, or horseradish to vary marinade flavor.

Mix honey, mustard, or sesame seeds in Crazy Charley's marinade to add sweet, tart, or texture to the marinade. Crazy Charley's marinade is great by itself, but sometimes I want a specific taste to dominate so I add the spice or herb to it. (Also adds nutritional value.)

To cut down on marinating time, use a Cajun injector (or large animal 2 ounce syringe from veterinary supply). Inject marinade deeply into whole chicken, turkey, roasts, and wild game. Let stand for 2 minutes; rub meat with a seasoning, such as Cajun powder, and roast, deep-fry, or cook meat as desired. Marinate in minutes, not hours, with injection. (Phone toll free 877-862-2586 [877-toCajun] to order your Cajun injector; includes instructions.)

Marinate vegetables like zucchini, onion, asparagus, and eggplant and barbecue, sauté or stir-fry.

MEAT KEBABS

3 lb. lamb, beef, pork, or chicken, in 2 inch cubes (or a combination
   of meats)
12 small onions

3 green peppers cut into quarters
1 c. Crazy Charley's marinade

Cover meat with marinade. Keep in refrigerator overnight or a minimum of 5 hours. Drain and reserve marinade. Lace meat cubes alternately with onions and bell peppers on 6 to 8 inch skewers. Place skewers on broiler pan and place 3 inches from heat. Broil for 20 minutes or until meat and vegetables are tender. Turn skewers several times, basting with marinade. (For out door barbecuing or grilling, place skewers on grate over medium-hot fire and follow directions for broiling.) Serves 6. Serve with Dirty Rice.

Lagniappe: Mix leftover marinade with 1 cup of Crazy Charley's Cajun BBQ; simmer for 10 minutes. Let diners add it to their meats.

DIRTY RICE

3 $^1/_2$ c. chicken stock
$^1/_2$ c. Crazy Charley's marinade
1 c. diced onion
3 cloves minced garlic
3 ribs chopped celery
1 tsp. Cajun powder (or use salt and black and cayenne peppers)
1 chopped bell pepper
2 Tbsp. olive oil
2 cups long grain rice

Bring canned or homemade chicken stock, marinade, and rice to a boil in a 2 quart saucepan. Sauté vegetables in olive oil in skillet until tender. Add sautéed vegetables to rice; simmer for 20 minutes. Fluff with a fork and serve as a side dish. Serves 6 to 8.

Lagniappe:

1 lb. chopped gizzards
$^1/_2$ lb. chopped chicken livers

Sauté in 2 tablespoons olive oil until brown. Add vegetables and cook until tender. Add to rice after rice has simmered 10 minutes; simmer until tender. This prevents overcooking the gizzards and livers. Use leftover meats and/or vegetables in Dirty Rice. Make ahead. Dirty Rice tastes better the second day. Called Dirty because of the "dirty" color.

STIR-FRIED PORK

1 lb. pork loin strips
1 diced red bell pepper
$^1/_4$ c. pecan pieces
1 tart green apple, cored and diced
$^1/_4$ c. marinade
6 diced green onions
$^1/_4$ c. marinade

Dust pork with Cajun powder or salt and pepper. Heat marinade in heavy skillet over medium heat add pork and stir-fry 2 minutes. Add rest of ingredients; cook and stir 2 minutes more. Serve with fresh cooked rice. Serves 4.

MARINATED ROAST

3 to 4 lb. top round, London broil, or tri-tip roast (or cut up chicken)
1 c. Crazy Charley's marinade

Marinate meat in the refrigerator for 6 to 12 hours covered. Pierce meat with fork. (Ziploc bags are great.) Turn meat several times while marinating in the refrigerator. Broil, bake, or grill as usual. Serve with roasted potatoes and garden salad. Serves 6. *Tastes great!*

ASPARAGUS-CHICKEN STIR-FRY

24 asparagus spears, cut in 2 inch diagonal pieces
2 chicken breasts, cut into thin strips
$^1/_4$ c. Crazy Charley's marinade
2 tsp. fresh grated ginger or 1 tsp. powdered
1 tsp. brown sugar

Heat marinade in wok or large fry pan. Add chicken strips to wok and sauté until done, stirring constantly. Add asparagus and ginger; sauté until tender crisp (3 minutes). Add sugar; stir until blended. Serve with rice. Serves 4.

PORK AND VEGETABLE BBQ WRAP

Briefly marinate 6 thin ($^1/_4$ to $^1/_2$ inch) slices of uncooked pork roast in

Crazy Charley's marinade for 15 to 20 minutes. Wrap each slice of pork around a bundle of blanched julienne cut vegetables (zucchini, green beans, asparagus, carrot, yams or ?). Secure each bundle with a toothpick and grill over electric or charcoal fire until pork and vegetables are cooked. Serve with salad and bread of choice. Makes 6 servings.

MARINATED CHICKEN WITH PASTA

1 chicken, skinned and cut up
1 c. marinade+3 c. water
1 (15 oz.) can stewed tomatoes
1 (8 oz.) can tomato sauce
2 tsp. oregano
1 Tbsp. chopped garlic
1 Tbsp. chopped parsley
1 Tbsp. chopped basil
1 Tbsp. dried onions
1 Tbsp. corn starch

Place chicken in a 2-quart pot. Add marinade and water; bring to a boil and simmer for 35 minutes, covered. Let cool. Drain off broth; save. Pull chicken from bones and place it in pot with broth. Add rest of the ingredients and simmer for 30 minutes. Spoon marinated chicken over a pound of your favorite pasta. Serves 6.

Lagniappe: When using dried or fresh garlic, parsley, and basil, reduce to 1 teaspoon and increase onion to $^1/_2$ cup when using fresh. Dried herbs season well. Fresh has a better aroma and texture then dried. Always use less dehydrated herbs and vegetables because they are concentrated.

SAUTEED GARDEN BURGERS

6 to 8 Garden or Veggie burgers, partially thawed
$^1/_2$ c. Crazy Charley's marinade

Heat an 8 or 9-inch skillet. Add half the marinade and heat until it bubbles. Place 4 burgers in skillet and cook 2 minutes; turn. Cook another 2 minutes or until tender. Repeat with remaining burgers. Serve on rolls with condiments of choice: mayonnaise, mustard, tomatoes, lettuce, and pickles are great! Serve with potato salad and chips. Serves 6 to 8.

MARINADE SALAD DRESSING

Add equal parts of olive oil to Crazy Charley's marinade; shake and use over fresh garden salads (assorted leaf lettuce, tomato, carrot, onion, cucumber, bell peppers, and jicama) or toss with diced tomato, lots of chopped fresh garlic and parsley, and place on lettuce leaves. Add small amounts of ginger, garlic, honey, or horseradish and blend well for the flavor you like.

ASPARAGUS SURF AND TURF JULIUS

1 lb. sirloin steak, cut into $^{3}/_{4}$-inch cubes
1 c. Crazy Charley's brand marinade
1 lb. peeled deveined medium shrimp (cooked or raw) or crawfish tails
$^{1}/_{4}$ c. chopped fresh mushrooms
1 tsp. salt
1 tsp. cayenne pepper
1 tsp. black pepper
$^{1}/_{2}$ lb. fresh asparagus, blanched
1 red bell pepper
2 oz. unsalted butter
4 cloves fresh garlic, minced
2 oz. blush wine
2 Tbsp. olive oil

Marinate steak for 2 hours. Cut asparagus into 1 inch pieces; remove tough ends. Julienne red bell pepper and mince the garlic.

In large sauté pan, melt butter on low heat. Add olive oil and garlic; cook until tender. Add steak; sauté over medium heat until browned. Add shrimp and simmer until pink. Add wine, red pepper, mushrooms, and asparagus; sauté until peppers are tender. Add seasonings and simmer 3 to 4 minutes. Serve with rice or as a filling for pita bread.

GRILLED LEMON GINGER ASPARAGUS

1 lb. fresh asparagus
1 c. Crazy Charley's marinade
1 tsp. ground ginger (or 1 Tbsp. fresh grated)
Juice of $^{1}/_{2}$ lemon

Mix marinade, ginger, and lemon juice; pour into a 2-quart Ziploc bag.

Add washed asparagus, tough ends removed, to marinade in bag. Marinate about 1 hour. Use a charcoal or electric grill. Place asparagus on grill about 4 inches from white hot coals or on medium electric heat. Grill about 6 minutes, turning several times. Grill asparagus as a side dish for grilled chicken, steaks, ribs, or fish. Serves 4 to 6.

Lagniappe: Marinated grilled vegetables are great. Use broccoli, celery, eggplant, onion, zucchini, or other vegetables. Skewer them for easy grilling. Serve with rice, angel hair pasta tossed in garlic-lemon butter, and/or your favorite grilled meat. Serve with garden salad and sweet French bread.

GRILLED LEMON GARLIC ASPARAGUS

2 lb. fresh asparagus
1 c. Crazy Charley's marinade (or quality soy based marinade)
$^1/_4$ c. minced fresh garlic
1 Tbsp. fresh grated ginger (optional)
Juice of 1 lemon

Mix marinade, ginger, garlic, and lemon juice in a 1 quart saucepan; bring to a boil. Pour over washed asparagus, tough ends removed (this will blanch the asparagus). Let asparagus marinate for 1 hour. Use a charcoal or electric grill. Place marinated asparagus on grill about 4 inches from white coals or medium electric heat. Grill about 6 minutes, turning several times. Serves 6 to 8.

Grill asparagus when you barbecue or grill. This spiced marinade is wonderful for marinating steaks, chicken, or fish. Marinate steaks and chicken for 6 to 8 hours fish for only 15 to 30 minutes.

FRIED RICE WITH SHRIMP

2 eggs
2 Tbsp. water
2 Tbsp. Olive oil
5 chopped green onion and tops
$^1/_2$ c. chopped green bell peppers
$^1/_4$ cup finely chopped celery
3 cups cooked long grain rice
$^1/_2$-1 lb. cooked small shrimp
3 Tbsp. Crazy Charley Marinade

Blend eggs and water; set aside. Heat oil in large skillet over medium heat. Add onions, bell peppers, and celery and cook until soft. Add egg mixture; scramble. Stir in rice. Gently fluff rice grains. Add shrimp and marinade. Cook, stirring until heated. Serves 6.

BOUDREAUX LOST HIS HAT

Boudreaux once spent days looking for his new hat. Finally, he decided that if he went to church on Sunday an sat at the back, during the service he could sneak out and grab a hat from the rack at the front door. So, on the following Sunday, Boudreaux went to church and sat at the back.

The sermon was about the Ten Commandments. He sat through the whole sermon and instead of sneaking out he waited until the preachin' was over an went to talk to the priest. "Father Pierre," Boudreaux say, "I came here today to steal a hat to replace the one I lost. But your sermon, the Ten Commandments make me change my mind, yea."

Father Pierre say, "Bless you my son. Was it when I start to preach Thou shall not steal, that changed you heart?"

Boudreaux say, "May mon, it was the one on adultery. When you start to preach on that, I remember where I left my hat."

THE CAJUN'S DONKEY

One day a Cajun's donkey fell into an abandoned well. The animal cried piteously for hours as the farmer tried to figure out what to do.

Finally, he decided the animal was too old and the well needed to be covered up anyway; so it just wasn't worth it to him to try to retrieve the donkey.

He invited all his neighbors to come over and help him. They each grabbed a shovel and began to shovel dirt into the well.

Realizing what was happening, the donkey at first cried and wailed. Then, a few shovels full later, he quieted down completely.

The farmer peered down into the well, and was astounded by what he saw.

With every shovel of dirt that hit his back, the donkey would shake it off and take a step up on the new layer of dirt.

As the Cajun's neighbors continued to shovel dirt on top of the animal, the donkey would shake it off and take a step up. Pretty soon, the donkey stepped up over the edge of the well and trotted off, to the shock and astonishment of everyone.

The Moral: Life is going to shovel dirt on you, all kinds of dirt.

The trick to getting out of the well is to stop wailing and not let the dirt bury you, but to shake it off and take a step up. Each of our troubles is a stepping-stone. We can get out of the deepest wells just by not stopping, never giving up! Shake it off and take a step up.

By the way, after he calmed down, the donkey kicked the crap out of the Cajun, who tried to bury him, which brings us to the second moral of this story: When you try to cover your a—, it will always come back to get you.

PIERRE AND BOUDREAUX FLY TO MARDI GRAS

Pierre and Boudreaux was flying Cajun Airlines to da Mardi Gras.

Boudreaux was flying da plane, and Pierre was in da back foolin' wi' da cargo equipment and stuff. Da plane hit some turbulence and started bouncing around and Boudreaux got knock unconscious. Den da plane start driftin'. Pierre came run up to da front and Boudreaux was sprawl out all over da steerin' wheel.

Well, Pierre don't know nuttin' bout flyin' an he start go get panaky.

He grab da microphone and holla, "May Day! May Day! Dis is Cajun Airline 90210. Boudreaux, him knock unconscious and I don know nuttin bout flyin' dis plane!"

"Dis is da control tower," someone answer. "Don you worry bout nuttin. We gonna splain how you to land dis plane, step by step, ah gar-own-tee! Jus leave everything to us; fus, how high you are, an wha's you position?"

Pierre thought a minute, den say, "I'm five foot ten and I'm all da way to da front of da plane."

"No! No!" answer da tower. "What you altitude, and where you location?"

Pierre say, "Man, rat now ah got a po' attitude, and ah'm from Thibodaux, Laweezeeanna!"

"No! No! No!" came an exasperated voice. "Ah need to know how many feet you got off da groun' an' how you plane in relation to da airport!"

Pierre, he start to panic by dis time. He say, "Countin' Boudreaux's feets and mine togedder, we got fo' feet off da groun' and I don believe dis plane related to you airport!"

A long pause—dee silence was deafanin'.

"We need to know who you next of kin . . . "

FISHING WITH BOUDREAUX

Boudreaux was stopped by a game warden in South Louisiana recently with two buckets of fish leaving a bayou well known for its fishing.

"Boudreaux, do you have a license to catch those fish?"

Boudreaux replied to the game warden, "These are my pet fish."

"Pet fish?" the warden asked.

"Yes, sir. Every night I take these here fish down to the bayou and let them swim around for a while. I whistle and they jump back into their buckets, and I take them home."

"That's a bunch of hooey! Fish can't do that!"

Boudreaux looked at the game warden for a moment, and then said, "Here, I'll show you. It really works."

"O.K. I've got to see this!" The game warden was curious now.

Boudreaux poured the fish into the lake and stood and waited. After several minutes, the game warden turned to Boudreaux and said, "Well?"

"Well, what?" Boudreaux responded.

PIQUANTE/SALSA AND RECIPES

CRAZY CHARLEY PIQUANTE SALSA

The best piquante sauce in the world, with no fat or oil and very low in sodium and calories. Warning—this product is habit forming!

PIQUANTE/SALSA

Piquante/salsa, that's what we call our end of the garden sauce. The Spanish word for it is "salsa" and it simply means sauce. Many cultures make this type of sauce.

English speaking cultures call it "chile sauce" and used to make it with bell peppers instead of chile peppers. A small amount of Tabasco sauce was added. (1952 Kerr Home Canning Book's Chili Sauce recipe calls for $3/4$ teaspoon of Tabasco with 1 gallon of tomatoes, that's all the chile in the sauce. Nutmeg, curry, ginger, cinnamon, and mustard are spices in the recipe.) With the increased popularity of "hot sauces" the past 10 to 15 years, hot peppers are finding their way into many dishes that used to be bland. It is exciting to eat tasty hot peppers, the biting starts in the mouth and moves over the whole body and lingers for hours.

The Spanish explorers were looking for gold and spices for their King when they found chile peppers in South America. Explorers brought seeds back to Europe and from there, they spread to Africa and the Far East. A welcome addition to native foods in a time when it was hard to keep foods from spoiling. Salting, drying, and smoking helped to extend the life of vegetables and meats and powdered sugar made them palatable when they were not fresh. Chile pepper varieties have different flavors as well as heat. All are delicious.

Salsa, chili sauce, is the number 1 condiment in use today. It is a versatile sauce made from vegetables or fruit or a combination, with one thing in common, lotsa "peppers."

Good eating doesn't have to be painful. Select the chili sauce that pleases the tastes of you and your guests. People have unique taste buds and it takes the range of peppers available to get all taste buds to sizzle.

Crazy Charley makes his Grandmother's piquante/salsa in mild and spicy. The mild is mildly spicy. It has green jalapeno peppers, laced with Tabasco brand pepper sauce.

SUGGESTIONS FOR PIQUANTE/SALSA

Use in all your Mexican and Southwest recipes. You will find it is spiced and heated just right for tacos, burritos, spooned over grilled steaks, chicken, and "as a dip," it's a tortilla chip's best friend. Use celery in place of chips. You choose "hot or mild."

Make a quick snack by smearing piquante on a large flour tortilla and top with a few pieces of cheese. Fold in half and microwave 1 minute. Cut into pie shape wedges to serve.

Spoon piquante on an omelette before folding and top with cheese or visa versa. Use on the side with eggs, prepared any way.

Top fresh cooked beans, red, white, pinto or other with Piquante as a garnish and flavor enhancer, I GUARANTEE you'll be happy.

Replace $^1/_4$ of liquid in biscuits with $^1/_2$ cup of piquante and $^1/_2$ cup grated cheese. Nothing dull about biscuits.

The following recipes illustrate the versatility of salsa. The great flavor is complementary to many foods. It can be fresh ingredients, served cold or in hot dishes. *Got a chip?*

PIQUANTE SALSA RELISHES

1 (14 oz.) jar Charley's piquante salsa (hot or mild)
1 (15 oz.) can whole kernel corn
1 (15 oz.) can black beans

Mix all ingredients. Serve as an appetizer with chips or as a lagniappe with a meal. Tastes great with just corn or black beans.

PIQUANTE SALSA DIPS

Pour 1 jar of Charley's piquante salsa over an 8 ounce block of creamed cheese. Serve with a small knife and assorted crackers. To garnish, use fresh chopped parsley and green onions.

GOURMET SEAFOOD DIP
from Mara Wilcox

12 oz. cream cheese
3 Tbsp. mayonnaise
1 small onion, minced
2 Tbsp. Worcestershire sauce
1 tsp. lemon juice
1 cup Crazy Charley's Piquante (mild or hot)
1 chopped crab, shrimp or lobster meat or a combination

This is a layered dip. Mix cream cheese, Worcestershire sauce, mayonnaise, lemon juice, and onion. Spread on the bottom of a nice serving dish. Spread the piquante sauce evenly over the cream cheese mixture. Spread seafood over the piquante and sprinkle with parsley. Serve with corn or tortilla chips or cocktail crackers.

Lagniappe: Use low fat or fat free mayonnaise and cream cheese to make a low fat dip—less fat and still delicious.

This is the best dip you have ever tasted; I guarantee!

QUICK THOUSAND ISLAND DRESSING

1 c. Crazy Charley's piquante (mild or hot)
1 c. mayonnaise (low fat or fat free)
$^1/_4$ c. pickle relish (optional)
$^1/_4$ grated onion (optional)

Mix ingredients together. Serve over green salads, fresh baked fish, or as a dip with chips, crackers, or cut up fresh vegetables.

GRILL-MARINATED CHICKEN BREAST

Marinate 1 chicken breast per person for 2 to 5 hours. Grill over medium hot coals on indoor grill or in a heavy skillet with enough marinade to keep it moist until meat pulls from the bone.

Top deboned breast with:
Thin sliced Swiss cheese
Diced avocado
Sour cream
Sliced black olives

Lagniappe: Melt cheese on top of boned chicken breast in microwave, then add the rest of the toppings.

CAJUN PIQUANTE SALAD GOES SOUTH
from Marion Sartori

2 lb. ground beef
3 cans kidney or red beans
1 can pitted black olives

1 large onion, diced
1 bunch green onions, diced
$^1/_2$ lb. grated sharp Cheddar cheese
3 medium tomatoes, diced
1 jar Crazy Charley's piquante (hot or mild)
1 head lettuce
1 bag tortilla chips

Brown the beef in skillet; drain and cool. Drain beans and olives. Add beans, olives, onions, cheese, tomatoes, and piquante to beef in a large bowl. Toss until mixed. Place the lettuce on large platter. Arrange tortilla chips over lettuce and top with mixture. Top with sour cream, if desired. Serves 8.

Lagniappe: Exchange 1 can of beans for a can of whole kernel corn. Top with diced avocado and 1 cup of sour cream.

PIQUANTE RICE-BEAN CASSEROLE
from Joanne Ryno

1 lb. ground beef
1 jar Charley's piquante (hot or mild)
1 (11 oz.) Green Giant Mexican whole kernel corn
1 pkg. Lipton Spanish rice mixture
$1^1/_2$ c. water
1 tsp. chili
4 oz. or 1 c. shredded Monterey Jack cheese

Brown ground beef in large skillet; drain. Stir in piquante, corn, water, chili powder, and black beans; bring to boil. Stir in rice mixture; cover. Remove from heat; let stand 5 to 7 minutes or until liquid is absorbed.

Follow directions on Spanish rice mix. Fluff mixture with a fork and sprinkle with cheese. Cover; let stand 2 to 3 minutes, until cheese is melted. Serves 6 with green salad and tortilla chips.

For Spanish rice, use the following meatless jambalaya recipe:

1 c. chicken broth
1 c. rice
14 oz. piquante or quality salsa

Cover and simmer 20 minutes.

PIQUANTE CARROT PASTA SUPREME

2 Tbsp. olive oil
5 cloves minced garlic
3 large carrots, shredded
2 Tbsp. butter
1 lb. spaghetti or angel hair pasta
1 tsp. brown sugar
$^1/_4$ cup piquante/salsa
$^1/_4$ cup chopped fresh parsley

Heat olive oil in medium size skillet; add garlic. Simmer until garlic is tender; do not let it burn or brown. Add carrots and brown sugar and stir; simmer for 5 minutes. Cook pasta according to directions on the package; drain.

Add butter and salsa to the carrot mixture and simmer 5 more minutes. Toss carrot mixture with pasta; fold in fresh parsley. Serve with your choice of bread and green salad. Serves 6.

JAMBALAYA

According to the Acadian Dictionary (Rita and Babrielle Claudet, Houma, Louisiana, 1981) the word "jambalaya" comes from the French "jambon" meaning ham, the Africa "ya" meaning rice, and the Acadian language where everything is "a la." It is a rice dish highly seasoned and can be flavored with any meat or combination or seafood.

To modify jambalaya recipe, use 1 pound ground turkey (mix 2 heaped tablespoons sage and 1 teaspoon Cajun powder or salt and pepper with ground turkey and you have a great low fat breakfast sausage) and $^1/_2$ pound low fat smoked sausage or ham to reduce fat and calories. Eliminate meat to make vegetarian jambalaya. For seafood, add to rice after it's cooked. Use brown rice to add fiber and flavor. Crazy Charley's piquante adds just the right heat and flavors to the jambalaya. Select hot or mild piquante to use in your recipes.

CHARLEY'S QUICK JAMBALAYA

$^1/_2$ lb. breakfast sausage (country style)
1 lb. smoked sausage
1 c. chopped tasso (peppered ham)
$^1/_2$ c. chopped green and/or red peppers
1 c. chopped onions
3 ribs chopped celery
3 c. chicken broth or good stock
1 jar Crazy Charley's piquante of choice
2 c. long grain white rice
$^1/_2$ c. chopped fresh parsley for garnish
$^1/_2$ cup chopped green onions for garnish

Sauté first 3 ingredients in heavy 4 to 6 quart pot until browned; add olive oil if needed. Add the next 3 ingredients; stir over low heat until tender. Add uncooked rice; stir until coated. Add broth, piquante/salsa, and salt and pepper to taste; bring to boil. Cover and simmer for 20 minutes. Just before serving, lightly toss with fresh parsley and green onions as a garnish. Serve with coleslaw and bread. Serves 8.

ASPARAGUS JAMBALAYA

Charley cooked this at the Asparagus Festival, Stockton, California.

1 lb. smoked sausage, cut in $^1/_2$-inch pieces
$^1/_2$ c. chopped bell peppers
1 c. chopped onions
$1^1/_2$ c. asparagus, cut into 1-inch pieces
2 chopped celery ribs with tops
2 c. long grain rice
3 c. chicken broth or stock
1 (14 oz.) jar Crazy Charley's hot or mild piquante
1 tsp. salt
$^1/_2$ c. chopped green onions

Brown sausage in 4 to 6 quart pot; drain fat. Add peppers, asparagus, onions, and celery; simmer until tender. Add rice and stir until rice is coated with sausage and vegetables. Add broth, salt, and piquante; bring to boil. Cover and simmer for 20 minutes or until rice is tender. Let stand 5 minutes, covered. Fold in fresh green onion just before serving. Serve with French bread and garden salad. Serves 6.

QUICK PIZZA

Pizza crust
2 tsp. oregano
1 jar Charley's piquante hot or mild
$^1/_2$ c. chopped onion
$^1/_2$ c. chopped bell pepper
$^1/_2$ c. chopped mushrooms
$^1/_2$ c. chopped zucchini
$^1/_2$ c. chopped tomato
$^1/_2$ c. chopped pineapple
$^1/_2$ lb. diced ham
$^1/_2$ lb. smoked sausage, sautéed
$^1/_2$ lb. diced chicken
$^1/_2$ lb. ground beef
$^1/_2$ lb. breakfast sausage
$^1/_2$ lb. ground turkey, salted and peppered
2 cups grated cheese of choice—Jack, Cheddar, Mozzarella
2 heaping Tbsp. grated Parmesan cheese to garnish top

Crust can be sliced bread, French bread cut in half long ways, flour tortillas, a purchased crust, or a homemade crust of a simple bread dough recipe, rice, or ?. Flatten crust in a large pizza pan or cookie sheet. Preheated oven to 450 degrees. Spread piquante salsa over baked crust; sprinkle with 1 teaspoon oregano and choice of 1 to 5 veggies or fruit and 2 meats listed. Sprinkle remaining oregano and grated cheese and top with Parmesan. Bake 20 minutes in hot oven. Serves 4 to 5.

PIQUANTE SALSA CHEESE SQUARES
from Adelaide Marriott

1 jar Charley's piquante salsa of choice
$^3/_4$ lb. sharp Cheddar cheese or choice
3 eggs
$^1/_2$ c. low-fat milk
$^3/_4$ c. biscuit mix
Pinch of salt

Spread piquante in the bottom of a 9x13 inch baking pan. Grate cheese and sprinkle over piquante. Beat eggs; add milk, biscuit mix, and salt. Mix well. Bake in 350 degrees oven 30 minutes or until light brown and firm. Cool; cut into squares. Serve warm. Serves 8.

TORTILLA SOUP PIQUANTE

For a quick meal and a way to use the dregs of the tortilla chip bag:

1 (14 to 15 oz.) can chicken broth
2 (14 to 15 oz.) cans chicken chile with beans
1 (14 to 15 oz.) can whole kernel corn
1 c. Crazy Charley's piquante (hot or mild)
Tortilla chips

Place all the ingredients in a 3 or 4 quart saucepan. Bring to a boil and simmer for 5 minutes. Let it stand for a few minutes to allow flavors to marry. Serve in shallow bowls and top with crushed tortilla chips.

Lagniappe: Add left over precooked or canned chicken cut into bite-sizes.

A long time ago, I was a professional Girl Scout worker, training, leading, directing camps, assisting neighborhood organizations and managing the infamous cookie sales. (This is where I got my first Marketing experience.) I taught the leaders to make the "Girl Scout Soup" loosely based on the children's story, "Stone Soup" where the poor man put water and a stone in a pot over a fire and invited others to join him for a meal by adding whatever they had to contribute. A carrot, a potato, an onion, etc. was added by other poor and they soon had a large pot of soup, which they all shared. I got the idea for this Tortilla Soup from that story. It is quick and tastes good, better the second day after the ingredients have more time to marry. (Girl Scouts each added a can of soup of choice to a pot, it is always good.) *Recipe by Ruth*

BLACK BEAN DIP

Add 1 cup piquante to a 15 ounce can of black beans. Chill 2 hours.

Just before serving, top with:

1 c. sour cream
4 oz. can chopped ripe olives
$^1/_2$ c. chopped red or green sweet pepper

Serve with tortilla chips or fresh vegetables for dipping. Makes 2 cups.

LAYERED DIP DIPS SOUTH

15 oz. refried beans
2 (8 oz.) tubs avocado dip
16 oz. light sour cream
1 jar piquante salsa
8 oz. sliced olives, drained
2 c. shredded Cheddar cheese
$^1/_2$ c. chopped green onions

Layer ingredients in order given in deep glass bowl. Serve with tortilla chips. Serves 8 to 10.

NACHO DIP

In 1 quart saucepan, place:

1 (10 oz.) can Nacho cheese soup
1 c. shredded Jack cheese
$^1/_4$ c. milk

Over low heat, stir until cheese melts. Stir in piquante salsa (hot or mild). Serve in fondue pot with French bread chunks or fresh vegetables or serve over tortilla chips. Makes $2^1/_2$ cups.

SAUSAGE AND PIQUANTE/SALSA

To make tasso, pound coarse black pepper into large piece of ham before dicing.

1 lb. breakfast sausage (country style)
$1^1/_2$ c. diced smoked ham or tasso
$^1/_2$ c. chopped bell peppers
1 tsp. Cajun powder or to taste
1 c. chopped onions
$^1/_2$ c. chopped garlic
2 chopped celery ribs
2 c. long grain rice

3 c. chicken broth
12 oz. jar Crazy Charley's piquante (hot or mild),
  or any quality salsa

Brown all ingredients listed before long grain rice in a large skillet. Put rice, chicken broth and Piquante in a rice cooker or 10 cup sauce pan, add browned sausages and vegetables and bring to boil, lower heat to simmer, cover and cook for 20 minutes. Remove from heat and fold in $1/2$ c. chopped green onions with tops and $1/2$ c. chopped fresh parsley. Serves 6.

Use a salsa maker to chop vegetables fast and easy. The longer you spin, the finer the chop.

Lafayette is the largest city in Cajun country and the unofficial Cajun capital of Louisiana. Acadians settled this area by 1770 and named it Vermillionville. In 1884 the name was changed to Lafayette in honor of the famous Marquis.

A LOUISIANA RAIN STORM

One night, a torrential rain soaked southern Louisiana; the next morning the resulting floodwaters came up about 6 feet into most of the homes there. Mrs. Boudreaux was sitting on her roof with her neighbor, Mrs. Tribodaux, waiting for help to come. Mrs. Tribodaux noticed a baseball cap floating near the house. Then she saw it float far out into the front yard, then float back to the house; it kept floating away from the house, then back towards the house. Her curiosity got the best of her, so she asked Mrs. Boudreaux. Do you see dat dere baseball cap a floatin' away from the house, den back again? Mrs. Boudreaux said, oh yeah, das my husband; I tole dat coonass he gonna cut the grass today, come hell or high water.

A VISIT TO DALLAS

When I was 10 years old, mama took me to Dallas to visit her sister, Mary Sue. We were walking down the street and two cowboys come walking up the street towards us. They were bow legged from riding horses. I laughed and yelled out, "Mama, look at those men with the funny legs."

Mama was embarrassed and told me she didn't like that kind of talk, making fun of other people. Then she told me for my punishment I had to read Shakespeare for three hours when we got back to Aunt Mary Sue's. She said she wanted me to learn the respectable way to talk.

The next day, we were out walking again, and we saw the cowboys. I said to mama, "What manner of men are these that wear their legs in parentheses?" *Charley*

AUNT DORA

I think my Aunt Dora was the reason for the beginning of blonde jokes. She was a local beauty and won several local beauty contests. She was so dumb she took a ruler to bed to see how long she slept. She studied two days for a blood test. She tried to put M&M's in alphabetical order. She thinks Taco Bell is a Mexican phone company. She thought a quarterback was a refund. At the bottom of her application, she wrote Sagittarius. When her boss died the police asked her what he said before he died; she said he kept saying dial 911. The police asked her why she didn't. She said she was waiting for the rest of the number. She married a rich oilman; she wasn't so dumb after all. *Charley*

GUMBO AND RECIPES

CRAZY CHARLEY CREOLE FILE GUMBO
(SPICY AND MILD)

So far as we know, this is the only bottled file gumbo available. Packed in 16-oz. Mason jars, it took over a year to get this recipe just right. You add your own meat or seafood and eat it over rice or use it as a fantastic soup. Once you start eating this dish, you just can't seem to stop. This is the product old-time Cajuns are raving about.

GUMBO: COOKING
WITH CRAZY CHARLEY'S GUMBO

According to Paul Prudhomme in *The Prudhomme Family Cookbook,* gumbo is "a Cajun soup almost always containing a cooked roux and it is sometimes thickened with okra or gumbo file." It usually contains a variety of seasoned vegetables and meats or seafood and is served over rice. Many people top gumbo with gumbo file (pronounced gum-boe fee lay). Gombo fevi is the Cajun name for okra; brought to this country by African slaves who hid seeds in their hair. Okra is used as a thickener in gumbo and served as a vegetable, fried, pickled, steamed, and boiled.

Down the Bayou, by the Bayou Civic Club, Larose, Louisiana, 1984, says, "Gumbo is native to South Louisiana. The dish can be made in other parts of the country if you can find fresh okra and powdered sassafras. Gumbo is a great winter soup. It is said that there are as many different kinds of gumbo as there are cooks, handed down from generation to generation. It is always unique and delicious."

The cookbook *La Cuisine Creole,* New Orleans, 1885 states: "This is a most excellent form of soup and is an economical way of using up the remains of any cold roasted chicken, turkey, game, or other meats. Oysters, crabs, and shrimp may be added when in season, as all improve gombo. Never strain the gombo. Serve gombo with plain boiled rice." (Gombo: Gumbo—old language.)

"Encyclopedia Americana," volume 20, page 700, 1982, states that "gumbo or okra is a large garden annual (hibiscus esalentus, of the mallow family) grown for its edible pods. It is also known as gombo, gobo, and lady's fingers. A native of Africa (Bantu), okra has long been cultivated in many other warm regions. It grows to a height of 4 to 6 feet. The edible part of the okra is the immature fruit, a pod 3 to 8 inches long, which may be eaten as a fresh vegetable, but is most widely used in cooking to thicken soups and stews."

Okra grown in the U.S.A. is a hybrid bred to reduce the slippery or slimy quality. Cooking methods can also eliminate slime.

Select Charley's gumbo mild or spicy depending on the amount of heat you desire. Charley's gumbo is easy to prepare right from the jar. As a vegetarian dish, just heat and serve over rice. Make it personal by adding chunks of your favorite vegetables and simmer until vegetables are tender and have absorbed the wonderful spices in the gumbo. As a soup add 1 cup chicken broth to gumbo; simmer 10 minutes and serve.

To make the gumbo soup special, add chunks of chicken and/or a small amount of rice with a 15oz can of chicken broth and small chunks of smoked sausage. To make shrimp gumbo soup, add shrimp to gumbo base (16 ounce jar) with 2 cups chicken broth. Use fresh cooked chicken, shrimp, smoked sausage or leftover meats for your gumbo entree. Serve this main dish over a bed of brown or white rice. You can combine smoked sausage with seafood or chicken. Potato salad is the side dish of choice by Cajuns and Creoles. I didn't know why until I ate them together. They complement each other, contrasting the spice in the gumbo and the mild potatoes in the salad.

Charley's gumbo has been handed down in his family for generations. It is a Creole file gumbo. We use a roux made of oil and tomato paste, instead of the traditional roux made with oil and flour. It has file (fee-lay) powder is ground leaves from the sassafras tree. The file powder acts as a thickening agent, as does the okra and it also gives the gumbo that rich brown color. We use olive oil in our roux. The oil prevents the tomato paste from burning during the long cooking time needed to create the right flavor and color.

Some people make gumbo without the file powder and others make it without the okra. Charley's mother and grandmothers used both file powder and okra and a tomato base with tomatoes from their kitchen gardens. Charley's family used shellfish in their gumbo for company and chicken for family. There is no right or wrong way to make or serve gumbo. You can create tasty dishes in minutes using Charley's gumbo.

USES FOR CHARLEY'S GUMBO

As a vegetable soup, thin with broth. Add rice and serve with French bread or crackers.

Toss with your favorite pasta and sprinkle with cheese.

Mix it in white or navy bean soup to add thickness and flavor.

Add chicken, smoked sausage, and a cup of chicken broth. Serve over rice.

Add fresh fish, shellfish, 1 kind or a mixture; thin with chicken broth. Serve over rice, brown or white.

Spoon your completed gumbo into bowls. Place an ice cream scoop of cooked corn meal, polenta, or grits in the center. Serve. Yum!

Use as a filling for baked potatoes. Be creative; there are hundreds of uses.

NAVY BEAN SOUP (CHARLEY'S FAVORITE SOUP)

1 lb. navy or white dry beans
2 to 4 oz. ham, bacon, or sausage
1 large onion, cut into large pieces
2 ribs celery, cut into large pieces
$^1/_2$ chopped green bell pepper
Salt, pepper, or Cajun powder to taste
1 Tbsp. chopped fresh parsley
1 c. Crazy Charley's gumbo of choice

Clean the beans and rinse. Bring to boil in a 4 qt heavy pot. Boil for 5 minutes, let set for 10 minutes. Drain off water and cover with fresh cold water, 2-3 inches above level of beans. Add the rest of the ingredients (except gumbo). Bring to a boil; lower heat and simmer for 2 hours or until beans are tender. Add gumbo and bring to boil. Turn off heat and let set for 5 minutes. Stir in fresh chopped parsley. Serve with sweet French bread. Serves 4 to 6.

Lagniappe: Add more ham or sausage for a meatier soup. This can be served as a first course with sausage jambalaya and a garden salad.

ROYAL SEAFOOD COURTBOUILLON

Don't let the long list of ingredients keep you from making this bouillon. You probably have most of them in your pantry and the finished product is delicious. You might want to double the recipe and save some for another day. Great the second day.

$^1/_4$ cup flour
$^1/_4$ cup olive oil
$^3/_4$ cup chopped onions
$^3/_4$ cup chopped green bell peppers
3 cloves minced garlic
$^1/_2$ tsp. crushed red pepper
1 cup Crazy Charley's gumbo
$^1/_2$ cup Crazy Charley's Cajun sauce
$^1/_2$ teaspoon salt
3 bay leaves
2 cups chicken or clam broth
$^1/_2$ cup dry white wine
4 thin slices lemon

2 Tbsp. chopped fresh parsley
2 lb. fresh fish, oysters, shrimp, or a seafood combination

In a 4 to 6 quart Dutch oven, stir together the flour and oil until smooth. Make roux by cooking over medium heat for about 20 minutes, stirring until roux is medium dark. Add the onion, bell pepper, celery, and garlic. Cook for 15 minutes or until tender, stirring often. You may need to add a small amount oil if mixture is too dry.

Stir in the red pepper, gumbo, barbecue sauce, salt, bay leaves, and broth. Bring the mixture to simmer again and simmer, uncovered, for about 30 minutes. Stir in the wine, lemon, and parsley. Bring the mixture to a simmer and add the seafood. Simmer 5 minutes. Turn off the heat and let the bouillon stand, covered, for 10 minutes. Serve over rice with potato salad and sweet French bread. Serves 4 to 6.

CHICKEN GUMBO SOUP

2 c. chicken broth or stock
$^1/_2$ c. long grain rice
$1^1/_2$ lb. chicken, in bite-size portions
$^1/_2$ lb. smoked sausage, cut in $^1/_4$-inch rings
16 oz. jar Crazy Charley Gumbo (mild or spicy)

Combine chicken broth, rice, and gumbo in a two-quart saucepan. Bring to boil; cover and simmer 20 minutes. Sauté sausage rings in 1 tablespoon oil until brown; add chicken. Mix until blended with sausage. Add meat to gumbo mixture; bring to boil and let stand 5 minutes. Serve with fresh sweet French bread for a winter lunch or as a first course for a delicious meal. Serves 8.

CHICKEN GUMBO AS AN ENTREE

1 jar Crazy Charley Gumbo (mild or spicy)
1 cup chicken broth
1 lb. cooked chicken, cut into bite-size pieces
$^1/_2$ lb. smoked sausage, cut into small pieces
2 cups cooked long grain rice

Pour gumbo into a 3 to 4 quart pan over high heat. Add chicken broth and bring to a boil. Place the chicken and sausage in a lightly oiled skillet and lightly brown. Add meat to gumbo and simmer for 10 minutes to marry flavors. Place cooked rice in a shallow soup dish and ladle prepared gumbo over the rice. Serve with potato salad as the Cajuns do or a tossed green garden salad. Serves 3 to 4.

To make a medium spicy gumbo for 6 to 8, mix a jar of mild with a jar of spicy gumbo. Double the amount of meat added.

SHRIMP GUMBO AS AN ENTREE

1 jar Crazy Charley Gumbo (mild or spicy)
1 to 1^1/$_2$ lb. peeled shrimp
1 cup chicken or vegetable broth
2 cups cooked long grain rice

Place the gumbo in a 3 to 4 quart saucepan. Add the shrimp and bring to a boil. Simmer 5 to 8 minutes; let stand for a few minutes. Place rice in a shallow soup bowl; ladle shrimp gumbo over the rice. Serve with tossed green garden salad or potato salad.

IN A BAR CELEBRATING

One day Boudreaux and Thibodaux were in a bar celebrating. The bartender asked, "What are y'all celebrating?"

Boudreaux said, "Hey, cher, me and Thibodaux here put a puzzle together and it only took us two years!"

The bartender said, "Well, don't you think that is a long time to put a puzzle together?"

Boudreaux and Thibodaux said, "No, not really. Dat puzzle box said 6 to 11 years."

BOUDREAUX'S MISSING WIFE

Boudreaux was waiting by his house cause his wife was missing. Boudreaux hear a knock at the door, so he answers it.

His buddy Thibodaux is at the door. Thibodaux says, "Boudreaux I got good news and bad news. The bad news is we found your wife drowned in the lake. The good news is when we picked her up out the lake she had 3 dozen crabs holding on. So, if you bring some beer, we are going to have a crab boil."

BOUDREAUX AND CLARENCE

Boudreaux lived on one side of the bayou and Clarence lived on the other side of the bayou. They were arguing across the bayou. Boudreaux tells his wife, "Beb, today is going to be the day that I will settle it with Clarence."

So Boudreaux gets in his truck, drives to the bridge to cross the bayou. Boudreaux looks up at the sign on the bridge, reads it, then turns around and goes back home.

Boudreaux's wife says, "Hey, Boudreaux, did you solve dat problem with Clarence?"

Boudreaux says, "No, Beb, they had a sign on the bridge that said Clearance 13 feet 3 inches, so I decided to leave him be."

THIBODAUX GETS A LOAN

Thibodaux walks into a bank in New Orleans and asks for the loan officer. He says he is going to Europe on business for two weeks and needs to borrow $5,000. The bank officer says the bank will need some kind of security for the loan, so the Cajun hands over the keys to a new Rolls Royce parked on the street in front of the bank. Everything checks out, and the bank agrees to accept the car as collateral for the loan.

The bank's president and its officers all enjoy a good laugh at the dumb Cajun for using a $250,000 Rolls as a collateral against a $5,000 loan. An employee of the bank then proceeds to drive the Rolls into the bank's underground garage and parks it there. Two weeks later, the Cajun returns, repays the $5,000 and the interest, which comes to $15.41. The loan officer says, "Mister, we are very happy to have had your business, and this transaction has worked out very nicely, but we are a little puzzled. While you were away, we checked you out and found that you are a multimillionaire. What puzzles us is, why would you bother to borrow $5,000?" The Cajun replied . . .

"Where else in New Orleans can I park my car for two weeks for only $15.41?"

ONE SUNDAY IN CHURCH

A young child was "acting up" during the morning worship hour. The parents did their best to maintain some order in the pew but were losing the battle. Finally, the father picked the kid up and walked quickly up the aisle. Just before reaching the safety of the foyer, the little one called out loudly to the congregation, "Pray for me! Pray for me!"

After receiving his punishment, the father overheard his son praying, "Lord, if you can't make me a better boy, don't worry about it. I'm having a real good time just like I am."

WE ATE WHAT WE CAUGHT

I love the outdoors, and because of my passion for hunting and fishing, my family used to eat a lot of wild game. So much, in fact, that one evening as I set a platter of fried catfish on the supper table, my daughter looked up and said, "Dad, it sure would be nice if pizza lived in the swamps."

ILLEGAL COCK FIGHTS

The Louisiana State Police received reports of illegal cockfights being held in the area around Lafayette, and duly dispatched the infamous Detective Desmoreaux to investigate.

He reported to his sergeant the next morning. "Dey is tree main groups in dis cock fightin'," he began.

"Good work who are they?" the sergeant asked.

Desmoreaux replied confidently, "De Texicans, de Cajuns, and de Mafia."

Puzzled, the sergeant nodded, "How did you find that out in one night?"

"Well," was the reply, "I went down and done seed dat cockfight. I knowed the Texicans was involved when a duck was entered in de fight."

The Sergeant nodded. "I'll buy that. But what about the others ?"

Desmoreaux intoned knowingly, "Well, I knowed de Cajuns were involved wen somebody bet on de duck."

"Ah" signed the sergeant, "and how did you deduce the Mafia was involved?"

"De duck won."

TEJON'S GIRL FRIEND

One night Tejon brought his new girlfriend home to meet his parents, and they were appalled by her appearance.

Later, the parents pulled Tejon aside and confessed their concern. "Dear," said the mother diplomatically, "she doesn't dress very nice, her blouse is so skimpy and that tight little skirt resting low on her hips showing her bellybutton and stomach is shocking."

"Oh please, Mom," replied Tejon, "if she wasn't nice why would she be doing 500 hours of community service?"

HANGING OUT WITH TEJON

Tejon liked to hang out at the local Winn-Dixie grocery store. The manager doesn't know what Tejon's problem is, but the boys like to tease him. They say, "he's two bricks short of a load." To prove it, the boys offer Tejon his choice of a nickel or dime. Tejon always takes the nickel because it is bigger. One day after Tejon grabbed the nickel, the store manager took him to one side and said, "Tejon, those boys are making fun of you. They think you don't know the dime is worth more than the nickel." "Well," said Tejon, "if I took the dime, they's quit doing it."

CAJUN POWDER, JALAPENO HEAVEN, AND RECIPES

CRAZY CHARLEY JALAPENO HEAVEN

Cajun Powder has a balance of salt and Cajun spices to give your meats, vegetables, eggs, and special dishes that Cajun flavor that tastes sooo good. Jalapeno Heaven pouring sauce, a jalapeno pepper sauce, begins where other pepper sauces leave off. Made from red, ripe jalapenos, it is a delicious medium-hot red sauce. Use it on meats and seafood, as a seasoning in your cooking, on the grill, or as a wing sauce.

CRAZY CHARLEY'S CAJUN POWDER

Here it is, folks, a seasoned salt that will give all your foods that great Cajun taste, made with salt, onion, green onions, cayenne pepper, garlic, and other natural spices. It is a unique blend of spices. Packaged in Louisiana, it's a long time favorite seasoning of Cajuns. This comes in a 7 ounce shaker.

The secret to the best foods you can eat is in the seasonings. Rub Cajun powder or sprinkle on chicken, beef, pork roasts, chops, potatoes, and vegetables with Cajun powder before roasting, grilling or barbecuing.

Use Cajun powder as a sprinkle in place of salt and pepper for great Cajun flavors. You can cut your salt 35 to 50% using Cajun powder. Sprinkle in a pot of beans, on eggs, in meat loaf, on popcorn, in casseroles, or ?? Cajun powder is made with natural ingredients, no anti-caking agents, MSG, sugar, or preservative. Ask for it by name at your grocers or order it on the web.

STANDING BAKED POTATOES

4 medium well shaped baking potatoes cheese
2 tsp. Cajun powder
2 to 3 Tbsp. melted butter or Butter Buds
2 to 3 Tbsp. chopped fresh parsley or thyme or substitute dried herbs
4 Tbsp. grated Cheddar cheese
1$^1/_2$ Tbsp. Parmesan cheese

Scrub potatoes (peel if skin is tough); rinse. Cut each potato in thin slices to within $^1/_2$ inch of complete cut. Place potato between 2 knives to prevent cutting through. Put potatoes in baking dish; pull slices apart slightly. Drizzle with melted butter or spray with Pam and sprinkle with Cajun powder. Bake potatoes at 425 degrees for about 50 minutes. Sprinkle with cheeses and return to oven. Bake until cheese melts and potatoes are soft. Serves 4.

Use zucchini or other vegetable; great as a side dish.

Lagniappe: Make this low fat with Butter Buds. Mix 1 package with $^1/_2$ cup hot water. Use as you would melted butter.

OVEN FRENCH FRIED POTATOES

Love French fries but not the fat? Here's what you've been waiting for. Use fresh cut scrubbed potatoes with skins on or off as you wish or frozen French fries prepared for cooking. Cut potatoes any size; the larger the pieces, the longer they must bake.

Wash potatoes or lightly sprinkle frozen potatoes with water or drizzle with melted butter or spray with a butter flavored cooking spray such as Crisco or Pam. Spread (skin down) on a cookie sheet or large baking pan and sprinkle with Cajun powder. Bake in preheated 425-degree oven. Bake until they feel soft inside when poked with fork.

For spicier fries, remove from oven after 10 minutes; turn potatoes. Sprinkle with Cajun powder. Return to oven following directions. For crispier fries, beat 1 egg white; toss dried cut potatoes in egg white. Sprinkle with Cajun powder and bake. Allow 1 potato per serving.

SEASONED COUNTRY FRIED POTATOES

1 medium potato per person (4 to 6)
1 green bell pepper
1 medium onion
3 to 5 cloves garlic
2 to 4 tsp. Crazy Charley Cajun powder
3 Tbsp. fresh chopped parsley
2 Tbsp. olive oil, or oil of choice

Scrub potatoes with vegetable brush; if you don't have one send a dollar and we'll send you one. Slice potatoes into thin ($^1/_4$ inch) rounds. Julienne (match like sticks) the bell pepper and onion, slice the garlic in thin slices, and chop the parsley or use 1 teaspoon dried parsley. Set aside.

In a deep skillet, heat the oil to hot or 375 degrees. Toss the potato rounds into the oil and toss until coated. If fat is not an issue in your diet, increase oil to 4 tablespoons. Cook on high heat until some are browned lightly. Add the peppers and onions and sprinkle on Cajun powder (if using dried parsley or garlic, add now) and toss until mixed with potatoes. Turn heat down and place a lid on the skillet and cook for 8 minutes, tossing occasionally, or until potatoes are done. If the mixture is very dry, add a little water to moisten.

When potatoes are almost soft, add fresh garlic and parsley and toss to mix. Let simmer for about two minutes. Great as a side dish for fish, beef, pork, chicken, or breakfast eggs.

CHARLEY'S POTATO SALAD

There are as many recipes for potato salad as there are cooks. Here is Charley's recipe.

> **4 to 5 medium russet potatoes**
> **4 hard-boiled eggs, chopped**
> **$^1/_2$ c. grated sweet pickles or pickle relish**
> **$^1/_2$ to $^3/_4$ cup mayonnaise**
> **1 tsp. prepared mustard**
> **1 Tbsp. sugar**
> **2 tsp. Crazy Charley Cajun powder**
> **$^1/_4$ c. fresh chopped parsley**

Scrub potatoes; leave skins on or peel as desired. Cut into bite-size cubes. Put 4 to 6 cups water into a 4 quart pan; add sugar and bring to boil. Place cubes of potatoes into boiling water and boil 6 to 8 minutes or until tender. Turn potatoes into colander and drain. Put potatoes back into pan. Add the chopped eggs and toss to mix with the potatoes. Add the rest of the ingredients and mix well. Add additional salt and pepper to taste. Prepare the salad several hours before serving, so the flavor can penetrate throughout the ingredients while chilling in the refrigerator. Serve with Gumbo, barbecued meats, or your favorite sandwich or Poor Boy. Makes 6 servings.

Lagniappe: Add $^1/_2$ cup chopped onion and/or celery.

CAJUN COLE SLAW

> **2 c. shredded cabbage**
> **1 c. shredded red cabbage**
> **1 c. shredded carrots**
> **$^1/_2$ c. raisins**
> **$^1/_2$ c. mayonnaise**
> **1 Tbsp. white or balsamic vinegar**
> **1 Tbsp. sugar**
> **1 tsp. Cajun powder or salt and pepper to taste**
> **$^1/_2$ tsp. Tabasco or to taste**

Place first 4 ingredients in medium bowl and mix. Place mayonnaise and seasonings in small bowl and mix. You may decrease or add amount of seasoning to suit your taste. Stir into cabbage mixture and mix well. Chill until time to serve. Serves 6.

BLACKENING SEASONING MIX

Use Crazy Charley Cajun Powder to make blackening seasoning mix: Mix 1 heaping tablespoon Cajun Powder and 1 heaping tablespoon ground black pepper together. For a hotter seasoning, mix in 1 level teaspoon ground cayenne pepper.

MAKE YOUR OWN BLACKENING SEASONING MIX

Blend:

- 1 Tbsp. paprika
- 2 tsp. salt 2 tsp.
- 1 tsp. onion powder
- 1 tsp. cayenne pepper
- $^1/_2$ tsp. ground white pepper
- 2 tsp. black pepper
- $^1/_2$ tsp. thyme
- $^1/_2$ tsp. oregano

RECIPE FOR BLACKENING

Blackening season mix
2 sticks butter (unsalted is best)
6 serving size pieces of firm fleshed fish like tuna, salmon, shark, snap per, sturgeon, and of course, redfish, beef tenderloin or sirloin, pork, chicken or hamburger patties

Melt the butter in a separate pan. Mix seasonings together in a small bowl. Heat a cast iron skillet until very hot. Pat fish or meat dry with a paper towel. Dip fillet or meat in melted butter and sprinkle seasoning mix evenly on both sides. Place in hot skillet and cook about 2 minutes on each side. Remove to serving plate and spread 1 teaspoon butter over blackened meat. Serve with standing Baked Potatoes, rice or Seasoned Country Fried Potatoes, choice of vegetable, green salad, and French bread. Accept the kudos. Serves 6.

SALMON BALLS

One of Charley's childhood favorites

    1 (15 oz.) can salmon, juice and all
    1 baked potato, mashed
    $^{1}/_{4}$ c. soda cracker crumbs
    $1^{1}/_{2}$ tsp. Cajun powder
    2 cloves garlic, minced
    1 egg, beaten
    Yellow corn meal for coating
    Vegetable oil for frying

Mix all ingredients, except the corn meal and the vegetable oil, until well blended. Heat a skillet with 1 inch oil to 375 degrees. Roll mixture the size of an egg into corn meal until coated. Fry in hot oil; turn when brown. Drain on paper towel. Serve with cocktail sauce and Cole Slaw. Serves 4.

SEAFOOD COCKTAIL SAUCE A LA FELIX

In 1948 my father took me to Felix's Oyster Bar on Bourbon Street in New Orleans and initiated me into the heavenly repast of devouring oysters on the half shell. Before we began eating the little morsels, Dad taught me how to concoct a wonderful cocktail sauce for oysters and shrimp. One can vary the heat in this product by changing the amount of Tabasco sauce or horseradish.

    1 c. catsup
    1 tsp. Tabasco pepper sauce
    1 tsp. Worcestershire sauce (I prefer Lea & Perrins)
    2 tsp. prepared horseradish
    Juice of $^{1}/_{2}$ lemon
    Salt and pepper to taste

Mix well and *shazam*, y'all, a wonderful sauce fit for a king! Use this sauce on all your seafood.

FRIED CATFISH

You will need 4 to 6 pieces freshwater catfish fillets.

Four 6-8 ounces catfish filets
Fish fry (I make my own* or use Cajun Land Fish Fry)
1 large egg
$^1/_2$ c. milk
1 tsp. Cajun seasoning
Vegetable oil or olive oil for frying

Beat egg; add milk and beat until well blended. Soak catfish fillets in egg mixture for 1 to 2 minutes, until all pieces are soaked. Dredge each fillet in fish fry until coated on both sides. I like to use a bag for dredging; less messy and it does it well.

Heat a skillet to 350 to 370 degrees with vegetable oil to moisten the skillet for sautéing fish or $^1/_2$ inch deep to fry. Lay fish flat in skillet and cook until browned, about 8 minutes. Turn and cook for another 6 minutes or until browned. Serve with hush puppies and coleslaw. Serves 4.

*Fish fry: Make your own fish fry by placing 1 c. cornmeal in a blender and blending until it has the consistency of flour. Add 1 tsp. Cajun powder, or quality Cajun or Creole seasoning, or a mix of salt, cayenne pepper, black pepper, onion powder, garlic powder, and a dried herb (oregano, basil, dried onion or green pepper—use about 4 parts salt and pepper to other seasonings). Be sure to use onion and garlic powder, not onion or garlic salt. The powders do not have salt in them; they are just dried onion or garlic.

Lagniappe: Use this recipe for cod, mahi mahi, or other fresh fish or sliced vegetables such as sweet potatoes, zucchini, or eggplant. Roll in fish fry and sauté, fry, or grill.

JALAPENO HEAVEN
(Pouring sauce by Crazy Charley)

By popular demand: "Where is your pepper sauce?" customers asked. I told them we consider Tabasco sauce our pepper sauce of choice. After all, our products are heated by Tabasco. Charley says his mother started putting Tabasco in his bottles with he was 6 months old and he's been hooked on the sizzle of Tabasco pepper sauce ever since.

Our customers explained they had hoped for a pepper sauce that was more than just peppers, salt, and vinegar, a unique pepper sauce, more robust flavor like our other products. After years of nagging, Charley and Paul, our canner, got busy one day and at day's end, they had Jalapeno Heaven, a sauce that begins where other pepper sauces leave off. Made with red vine ripened jalapenos, full of flavor, mellow, sweet, nutty, and 9X the vitamin C (than green peppers) a delicious medium hot sauce. Thanks, Charley and Paul.

Jalapeno Heaven made its debut at the 1997 Fiery Food Show in Albuquerque with samples only. Labels had not been made. All tasters found the sauce uniquely different. Ron Smith from Ventura, California, remarked, "Wow, this sauce is so good I could just pour in on." We all laughed with the words "pouring sauce" ringing in our ears. It was true; the wonderful full flavor of ripe jalapeno cried for pouring, on hamburger, steaks, fish, eggs, Mexican and Southwest dishes, as a dip, and more.

Mix equal parts of horseradish, and it's a great seafood sauce. We hope you'll write and tell us how you use it and send your recipes. We still use Tabasco Brand pepper sauce in our Cajun sauce (BBQ), marinade, gumbo, and piquante salsa. It is part of the original recipes; we can't cook them without it. We have started using Jalapeno Heaven as the seasoning in beef stew, to add spice and more flavor to spaghetti sauce, as a wing sauce, and a grilling sauce.

HOW TO BOIL SHELLFISH

When boiling shellfish, please put some seasoning in the water. It will make the shellfish taste so much better. Use a crab boil purchased at your super market by Zatarain's, Tony Chachere's, Cajun Land, or make your own.

1 Tbsp. mustard seed
1 Tbsp. coriander seed
4 bay leaves, broken into pieces
3 tsp. Cajun Powder

1 tsp. allspice
1 tsp. thyme

Place all ingredients in cheesecloth and tie in bundle. Place seasoning mix bundle in 3 quarts boiling water for 30 minutes to season water before adding shellfish (or use powdered mustard and coriander add rest of ingredients and boil for 5 minutes then add shellfish to boiling water). I like to add one lemon, cut into rings, into boiling water with the spice mix. Bring to rapid boil; add 2 pounds shrimp or crawfish (crab). Bring water back to a boil; turn off heat and remove shrimp or crawfish. For crab, let it boil for 2 to 3 minutes before removing from heat. Cover with ice to quickly cool. Refrigerate until ready to use. Serve shellfish cold or hot, in Jambalaya, Gumbo, Etouffee, or in salads. (Place ingredients in a coffee grinder to make a powder which will dissolve in boiling water instantly for a quicker seasoning.)

BRAISED CHICKEN WINGS

$^1/_2$ c. marinade
2 green onions cut in 1 inch pieces
$^1/_2$ c. water
15 chicken wings, separated at the joints
1 tsp. Cajun powder

Combine all ingredients in a medium saucepan. Cover; bring to a boil. Simmer 30 minutes. Uncover; simmer 15 minutes longer, basting frequently. Serve hot or cold. Use Crazy Charley's Cajun Sauce as a dip for the wings (hot or mild).

BLACK-EYED PEAS AND RICE

1 Tbsp. Olive oil
1 c. diced red or green bell pepper
$^1/_2$ c. diced onion
$^1/_2$ c. diced celery
2 tsp. minced garlic
1 tsp. Cajun powder
$^1/_2$ tsp. salt
1 cup dried black-eyed peas
3 cups water
$^3/_4$ cup uncooked rice
$^1/_2$ chopped green onion

In a large pot, heat oil over medium heat. Add diced pepper, onion, celery, garlic, Cajun powder, and salt. Cook stirring until softened for 3 to 4 minutes. Stir in black-eyed peas. Add 3 cups water; bring to a boil. Cook, uncovered for 30 minutes. Stir in rice; cover. Reduce heat to medium-low; cook until all liquid is absorbed, 15 to 20 minutes. Before serving, stir in green onions. Serve in bowls. Makes 6 servings.

YOGURT-CAJUN POWDER DRESSING

$^1/_4$ c. plain yogurt
1 Tbsp. Dijon mustard
2 tsp. cider vinegar
$^1/_2$ tsp. Cajun Powder or to taste
2 tsp. sugar

Combine all ingredients, mix well, and use on your favorite green salad.

POTATO-CRAB CAKES

$^1/_2$ lb. potatoes, cooked and mashed
3 cloves minced garlic
1 Tbsp. fresh chopped chives*
1 Tbsp. fresh finely chopped tarragon*
$^1/_2$ c. fresh corn, cooked and cut from cob
1 medium tomato, diced
1 egg, whipped until frothy
6 oz. fresh lump crabmeat
$^1/_2$ tsp. Cajun powder or to taste
$^1/_4$ c. corn flour or seasoned fish fry**
2 Tbsp. olive oil

Preheat oven to 375 degrees. To the mashed potatoes, stir in garlic and herbs.* Add corn and beaten egg and mix well. Add the crab and mix again. Season to taste with Cajun powder.

Form the mixture into 3 inch round cakes, about $^5/_8$ of an inch thick. Make cakes 5 inches in diameter to use as an entree. Dredge the cakes lightly with corn flour or seasoned fish fry. Heat the olive oil in a skillet and cook for three minutes on a side or until browned. Place the browned cakes in the oven and bake 10 minutes to finish cooking. Drain on paper towels. Serve these potato cakes as appetizers, a side dish with meat, or fish, or as a main course for 4 served with vegetables and a green salad.

*Use a scant tsp. if using dried chives and tarragon.
**Add Cajun powder to corn flour or fish fry to make a seasoned fish fry.

PAN BLACKENED MEDALLIONS
OF PORK TENDERLOIN

Chef Charley Addison cooked this at the Garlic Festival in Gilroy, CA.

16 oz. pork tenderloin, cut into bite-size pieces
^{1}/$_3$ cup blackening seasoning
1/2 cup unsalted butter
1 Tbsp. minced garlic
^{1}/$_3$ cup chopped fresh parsley

Blackening Seasoning:

1 tsp. paprika
1 tsp. white pepper
2 tsp. salt
1 heaping tsp. ground black pepper
1 tsp. onion powder
1 tsp. garlic powder
^{1}/$_2$ tsp. thyme
1 tsp. cayenne pepper
^{1}/$_2$ tsp. oregano

Or the fastest method for blackening seasoning:

1 heaping Tbsp. Crazy Charley's Cajun Powder
1 tsp. paprika
1 heaping Tbsp. ground black pepper

Dredge pork in the butter. Put Blackening Seasoning in paper or plastic bag and shake meat until well coated. Put in 400-degree iron skillet and sear about three minutes. Turn out on platter and sprinkle garlic and parsley over meat. *Wow!* This is good folks. Serves 4.

FISH MULLIGAN STEW

1 lb. any lean fish
4 large potatoes
2 large onions
6 c. hot water
$^1/_3$ cup uncooked rice
2 green peppers, diced
3 to 4 oz. diced bacon, ham, or salt pork
2 Tbsp. minced parsley
Salt and pepper or Cajun Powder to taste

Cut fish into chunks; slice potatoes and onions $^1/_2$ inch thick. Place in kettle; add water and bring to a boil. Add rice, green peppers, ham, bacon, or salt pork. Simmer about 30 minutes or until tender. Add parsley and a few slices of dry bread. Vegetables such as peas and/or corn may be added. Season to taste, bring to a boil. Serves 6 to 8.

CORN AND POTATO CHOWDER

$^1/_2$ c. cooked corn
2 c. diced potatoes
$^1/_2$ c. diced celery
1 Tbsp. butter
$^1/_2$ c. diced onions
$^1/_2$ c. diced onions
$^1/_2$ tsp. Cajun Powder
1 c. boiling water

Boil all ingredients in water until potatoes are tender. Add 2 cups hot milk which has been thickened with 1 tablespoon flour mixed in 1 tablespoon cold water. Heat until boiling. Serves 4 - 6.

SALMON BISQUE

2 Tbsp. olive oil
1 Tbsp. butter
1 small onion, minced
4 Tbsp. flour
1 tsp. Cajun powder

4 cups warm milk
$^1/_2$ cup cooked peas
1 cup canned/fresh salmon

Melt butter in olive oil; add onion and simmer 5 minutes -do not brown. Blend in flour and Cajun powder. Add milk gradually, stirring constantly. Remove skin and bone from salmon and rub through a sieve with the peas. Add to milk mixture; heat and serve at once. Garnish with chopped parsley and a squeeze of fresh lemon juice. Bisque should be smooth textured with a mild flavor of fish. Serves 4-6.

CAJUN CRAB AND SHRIMP PIE

$^1/_2$ c. chopped onion
$^2/_3$ c. chopped green peppers
1 cup chopped celery
2 cloves minced garlic
1 (2 oz.) jar pimientos, drained
2 Tbsp. olive oil
$1^1/_2$ tsp. Cajun Powder
$^1/_4$ cup chopped fresh parsley
1 can cream of mushroom soup
1 cup cooked crabmeat
3 cups hot cooked long grain rice
8 small pie shells or 1 large

Preheat oven to 400 degrees. In a medium skillet, sauté first 8 ingredients until vegetables are soft and well blended. Add soup and stir well. Fold in crabmeat, shrimp, and rice. Place in pie shells and bake for 20 minutes. Serves 8.

This can also be served as a main dish.

BLACK-EYED PEAS AND MUSTARD GREENS

3 large cloves minced garlic
1 (16 oz.) can diced tomatoes
10 oz. frozen black-eyed peas
$^1/_2$ cup dry white wine
2 Tbsp. brown sugar
1 tsp. mustard seeds
1$^1/_2$ lb. mustard greens
1$^1/_2$ tsp. Cajun Powder

Simmer garlic, tomatoes, peas, wine, sugar, and mustard seeds in medium size pot and simmer for 20 minutes. Cut greens into small pieces about 1 inch and add to pot and simmer 10 minutes longer. Substitute Swiss chard or collard greens. If fresh greens are used, cook them first until they are almost tender, then add as recipe suggests for frozen greens. Canned black-eyed peas can be used but they just need to cook long enough to blend with other ingredients. This makes a good side dish for any meat. Serves 8.

Lagniappe: Use sliced fresh or frozen okra in place of mustard greens.

SWEET POTATO BISQUE

2$^1/_2$ southern sweet potatoes
3 sweet apples
3 c. low fat chicken broth
$^1/_2$ c. dry white wine
$^1/_4$ tsp. cinnamon
$^1/_4$ tsp. nutmeg
$^1/_4$ tsp. ginger
$^1/_2$ tsp. Cajun Powder
3 Tbsp. finely chopped fresh chives or parsley

Cut sweet potatoes in halves lengthwise and place halves upside down in 9x13 inch baking pan. Peel, halve and core apples, add to pan with $^1/_4$ cup water. Bake in regular oven or microwave until sweet potatoes and apples are tender. 45 minutes in standard oven or 10-15 minutes in microwave oven. When cool remove and discard peel from sweet potatoes.

Place sweet potatoes and apples in blender with broth and blend until smooth. Pour the puree into a medium size saucepan. Add wine, spices and

Cajun powder and bring to a boil. Simmer for 15 minutes to blend flavors, stirring occasionally. Serve in bowls: garnish with chives or parsley. Serves 4-6.

SKILLET CHOPS AND RICE

4 pork chops
1 small can onion soup
1 can water
$^1/_2$ cup uncooked rice
$^1/_2$ cup chopped celery
$^1/_2$ cup chopped onion
$^1/_2$ cup chopped bell pepper
1 tsp. Cajun Powder

In a skillet, brown chops; season with Cajun Powder. Add celery, onions, and bell peppers and sauté until lightly browned. Add soup and water. Cover and cook 20 minutes or until chops and rice are tender. Serves 4.

This is an easy way to make an etouffee (smothered dish). Make this recipe with chicken or shrimp, using cream of mushroom soup.

TOSSED GREEN SWEET PEA SALAD

4 cups frozen or canned sweet peas, cook frozen as directed on pkg.
$^1/_2$ cup finely chopped onions
$^1/_2$ cup finely chopped celery
$^1/_4$ cup finely chopped green bell peppers
$^1/_4$ cup finely chopped red bell pepper
1 large head romaine lettuce, finely chopped
2 hard-boiled eggs, thinly sliced

Combine all ingredients except sliced eggs.

Make a creamy dressing by mixing in a medium bowl:

$^3/_4$ cup mayonnaise
1 Tbsp. sugar
1 tsp. fresh lemon juice
1 tsp. Cajun Powder
$^1/_4$ cup milk

Pour over salad; toss just until mixed. Garnish with sliced eggs and Cajun Powder. Serves 8.

RATATOUILLE

1 yellow onion
3 to 4 garlic cloves, minced
$^1/_2$ cup olive or canola oil
2 medium size eggplants (peel on), diced*
1 medium size red bell pepper, sliced $^1/_2$-inch strips
2 zucchini squash, diced
4 large Roma tomatoes, diced
1 tsp. Cajun Powder
1 Tbsp. tomato paste (optional)
1 medium size yellow bell pepper, sliced in $^1/_2$-inch strips

Sauté onions briefly in olive oil using heavy pan. Add eggplant and garlic, reduce heat after a few minutes. Add sliced bell peppers and cover, braising for 10 minutes. Add squash and tomatoes, herbs and seasonings and continue cooking for fifteen minutes, covered. Adjust seasonings before serving warm or hot.

Option A: Normally served as a vegetable side dish, Ratatouille can easily become the main event. The "meaty" qualities of eggplant combined with tomatoes, peppers and squash make this vegetable stew complete when accompanied by polenta or brown rice, or served as a sauce over penne pasta.

Option B: Slice sufficient eggplants (1 per 2 servings) in halves lengthwise. Remove some of the "meat," leaving $^1/_2$-inch sides, and roast the eggplant for half an hour in 350-degree oven. Stuff with Ratatouille and garnish with fresh basil.

*Soak diced or halved eggplant in salt water for 30 minutes before cooking.

FRIED EGGPLANT

1 large eggplant
1 egg
$^1/_2$ c. fish fry
2 Tbsp. olive oil or vegetable oil

Peel eggplant and cut into $1/2$-inch rounds. Place in bowl and cover with salted water (1 tsp. salt to each cup water). Let stand for 20-30 minutes. (The salt draws out the moisture and the bitter flavor and enhances the taste of the finished product.) Rinse eggplant in fresh water and blot with paper towels until dry.

Beat egg until frothy. Dredge each eggplant round in egg and lightly dust with fish fry. Let set until egg soaks up fish fry.

Heat oil in large skillet to 370 degrees. Place eggplant in oil and cook until brown and tender on both sides. Serve with a main course or as an appetizer. Serves 4. You can also use zucchini rounds; they do not need to be soaked in salted water.

Note: See the Fried Catfish recipe in this chapter for directions on making your own fish fry.

CORNBREAD AND PECAN DRESSING

4 c. crumbled cornbread
$1/2$ c. pecan halves, broken into quarters
2 tsp. dried sage
1 Tbsp. olive oil
6 to 8 oz. smoked sausage, diced
$3/4$ cup chopped onion
$3/4$ cup chopped celery
$1/2$ lb. frozen corn or 8 oz. canned whole kernels
2 tsp. dried sage
$1/2$ c. fat free chicken broth (enough to moisten)
1 tsp. Cajun powder or to taste
1 lb. fresh or frozen chopped mustard greens

Toast cornbread crumbs in toaster oven, stirring several times, until browned. Place pecan pieces in same oven and roast until lightly browned.

In a medium skillet, heat olive oil to medium heat; sauté onions, celery, and sausage until browned, 5 to 7 minutes. Remove excess liquid from chopped mustard greens. Add greens, corn, sage, and sausage and stir until blended. Mix in cornbread and enough chicken broth to moisten. Stir in pecans and Cajun powder. Spread dressing in a shallow $1^1/2$ quart baking dish, covered. Bake at 325 degrees for 12 to 20 minutes, until hot in center. Uncover and bake until top is browned, 10 to 15 minutes.

Make homemade cornbread or use a mix. Serve with sliced turkey or chicken pieces fried, baked, or roasted. Serves 6-8.

JALAPENO-RANCH SALAD DRESSING
(You won't believe this)

Charley and I sell a lot of our sauces at Home and Garden Shows, Arts and Craft shows, Harvest Festivals, and the like. At our last show, a very attractive young couple stopped by our booth and shared this story. The young lady wanted to lose 100 pounds before her wedding. She was successful because she ate Chicken Caesar Salads with a dressing made of equal parts of our Jalapeno Pouring Sauce and low fat Ranch dressing.

The taste is so wonderful she continues to make this dressing for her salads.

RECIPE FOR THE FISHERMEN
from the Laguna Madre Club in Port Mansfield, TX, submitted by Troy A. Nicholas

Fillets of trout, redfish, or other fresh fish
Dill weed, lemon pepper, and minced garlic
Olive oil for frying
Flour for dredging fish
Jalapeno Pouring Sauce, Trappey's, or any brand medium hot sauce

Marinate fish fillets (8 oz. per serving) for at least 20 minutes in pepper sauce which has been mixed with dill, lemon, and garlic. Dredge fillets in flour; fry in hot olive oil (350-375 degrees). Turn when browned and cook on other side. Serve at once; don't let it sit.

SUGAR BOWL

Thibodaux had 50 yard line tickets for the Sugar Bowl. As he sits down, a man (who apparently breached Secret Service security) comes down and asks if anyone is sitting in the seat next to him.

"Mais, no," says Thibodaux, "dat seat be empty, yeah." "That's incredible," said the man. "Who in their right mind would have a seat like this for the Sugar Bowl, the biggest sporting event of the year for LSU, the SEC champions, the first time since 1987, they make it to the Sugar Bowl, and then not use it?"

Thibodaux says, "Dat seat belong wit me, yeah. I wuz comin' with my wife, but she done pass on. Dis de first LSU football game we didn't came with each udder since we bin married in 1960."

"Oh...I'm sorry to hear that. That's terrible. But couldn't you find someone else—a friend or relative, or even a neighbor to take the seat?"

Thibodaux shakes his head sadly. "No, dey all at de funeral."

NO BREAKFAST UNTIL YOU DO YOUR CHORES

A little boy comes down to breakfast. Since they live on a farm, his mother asks if he had done his chores. "Not yet," said the little boy. His mother tells him no breakfast until he does his chores.

Well, he's a little mad, so he goes to feed the chickens, and he kicks the chicken. He goes to feed the cows, and he kicks a cow. He goes to feed the pigs, and he kicks a pig. He goes back in for breakfast and his mother gives him a bowl of dry cereal.

"How come I don't get any eggs and bacon? Why don't I have any milk in my cereal?" he asks.

"Well," his mother says, "I saw you kick a chicken, so you don't get any eggs for a week. I saw you kick the pig, so you don't get any bacon for a week either. I saw you kick the cow, so for a week you aren't getting any milk."

Just then, his father comes down for breakfast and kicks the cat half way across the kitchen floor. The little boy looks up at his mother with a smile, and says, "Are you going to tell him, or should I."

A PAIR OF ALLIGATOR SHOES

A young blonde was on vacation in the depths of Louisiana.

She wanted a pair of alligator shoes in the worst way, but was very reluctant to pay the high price the local vendors were asking.

After becoming very frustrated with the "no haggle" attitude of one of the shopkeepers, the blonde shouted, "Maybe I'll just go out and catch my own alligator so I can get a pair of shoes at a reasonable price."

The shopkeeper said, "By all means, be my guest, maybe you'll luck out and catch yourself a really big one!"

Determined, the blonde turned and headed for the swamps, set on catching herself an alligator.

Later in the day, the shopkeeper is driving home when he spots the young woman standing waist deep in water, shotgun in hand.

Just then, he sees a 9 foot alligator swimming quickly towards her. She takes aim, kills the creature, and with a great deal of effort, hauls it onto the swamp bank. Lying nearby were several more of the dead creatures.

The shopkeeper watches in amazement. Just then, the blonde flips the alligator or its back, and frustrated, shouts, "Darn, this one isn't wearing shoes either!"

"WHEN I DIE," SAID BROUX

Broux had worked all of his life and had saved all of his money and was a real miser when it came to his money. He loved money more than just about anything. Just before he died, he said to his wife, "Now listen. When I die, I want you to take all my money and put it in the casket with me because I want to take my money to the afterlife with me." And so he got his wife to promise him with all of her heart that when he died, she would put all the money in the casket with him. Well one day he died. He was stretched out in the casket, the wife was sitting there in black, and her friend was sitting next to her.

When they finished the ceremony, just before the undertakers got ready to close the casket, the wife said, "Wait just a minute!" She had a box with her, she come over with the box and put it in the casket. Then the undertakers locked the casket, and they rolled it away. So her friend said, "Girl, I know you weren't fool enough to put all that money in there with that man." She said, "Listen, I'm a Christian, I can't lie. I promised him that I was gonna put that money in that casket with him." "You mean to tell me you put that money in the casket with the man?" "I sure did," said with wife. "I wrote him a check!"

SIGNS IN A RESTAURANT

We practice safe cooking—we use condiments.

Do you want to talk to the man in charge or the woman who knows what's going on?

HOW ABOUT SOME SAUSAGE?

Sausage is any ground or chopped meat that is seasoned, spiced, and shaped, usually in a casing or round patty. Sausages may come cooked, uncooked, or cured. Curing processes include drying, smoking, and acidification (changing into an acid) and may be used to enhance the flavor, texture, and shelf life.

Sausage making transforms carcass trimmings and tough cuts of meat into valuable foods. (Look at the list of ingredients on the next sausage you buy—surprise!) Most sausage is made from beef or pork; however, the use of poultry has become popular. Other ingredients are added to the meat to season it before it is loaded into casings of flushed animal intestines or artificial casings made of collagen, cellulose, or plastics. There are hundreds of different kinds of sausages made all over the world. Most can be classified into one of the following six categories.

1. Fresh sausages are neither cooked nor cured with nitrates. Examples are Italian sausage, fresh pork sausage, and bratwurst. Pork predominates in fresh sausage marketed in link, patty, or bulk form. These must be fully cooked before eating.

2. Cooked sausages are fully cooked, not smoked, but maybe cured. They include liver sausage, blood and tongue sausage, and precooked bratwurst.

3. Cooked smoked and cured sausages are the most popular. They include frankfurters, bologna, cotto salami, and andouille usually made from pork or beef. They are not raw so can be eaten cold, heated, or cooked in dishes such as gumbo, jambalaya, or beans.

4. Semidry sausages are prepared by bacterial fermentation that converts added sugar to lactic acid. This enhances flavor, texture, and shelf life. Summer sausage, Thuringer, and Lebanon bologna are examples of semidry varieties, which are slightly dried and smoked.

5. Dry varieties of sausages are not usually smoked but are dried under carefully controlled conditions. Examples are pepperoni, Genoa salami, and hard salami.

6. Cooked meat specialties include loaf products made from cured or uncured meats that are cooked or baked in molds. Example are roast beef loaf, head cheese, and Dutch loaf.

Sausage was made in Babylonia about 1500 B.C. and later in Rome and Greece. Sausages were known to the people of these early times as "bacon," especially to the settlers who moved West during the expansion of the United States. Making sausages was a way to preserve meats for long travels and future use. Refrigeration and freezing of foods is a relatively modern capability.

During the Middle Ages, sausage making flourished in Europe. You can easily guess from the names where some sausages were developed, e.g., frankfurters—Germany, bologna—Italy, Genoa salami—Genoa, Italy. Black pudding, an ancient dish in England and Scotland, was made of oatmeal, suet, and hog's blood. During this time, the Italians, French, and Greeks perfected sausage making.

When Europeans, predominantly French and Spanish, settled in the American South, they ate what Native Americans ate—corn, squash, beans, wild turkey, fish, deer, and rabbit. They established herds of pigs, and pork became the main ingredient for their meals. The preservation of pork became a necessity. On plantations, smokehouses were erected, and homemade sausages flavored with sage and spices were smoked and stored.

Broussard, Louisiana, holds an annual Boudin Festival. Boudin blanc can be made with chicken, turkey, dove or other birds, crab, crawfish, squirrel, or rabbit. A sausage called boudin blanc ("white pudding") is also made in France, but it is nothing like the Cajun kind. In France it is a delicate sausage, with chicken, cream, and eggs in it. The Cajun boudin (pronounced "BOO-dan") is a sturdy sausage with pork, rice, onions, and spices. The Cajun people are frugal and added rice to boudin to stretch the meat. There is also a Cajun sausage called boudin rouge. It is a blood sausage and is very good, but it must be very fresh and is difficult to find.

Chuck Taggart tells about the availability of "hot boudin" in Acadiana (Cajun country) at grocery stores, gas stations, and little stands along the road. It is usually served in a casing, but if you make it at home you can serve it without the casing and it tastes just as good. In a casing it travels well and is easy to heat in a steam bath or microwave.

Ruth

BOUDIN BLANC

3 lb. boneless pork butt or shoulder roast
1 large onion
1 bunch parsley
3 ribs celery, chopped
2 bay leaves
1 tsp. cracked black peppercorns
3 c. uncooked long-grain rice
4 slices bacon

2 bunches green onions
2 medium yellow onions, chopped
1 Tbsp. minced garlic
1 lb. pork liver
1 Tbsp. salt
1 Tbsp. cayenne pepper
2 tsp. freshly ground black pepper
2 tsp. white pepper

Cut pork in large chunks. Cut onion in 8 wedges. Cut stems from parsley and reserve leaves. Place pork, onion, parsley stems, celery, bay leaves, and pepper in a 6-qt. saucepan.

Cover with water (at least 4 qt.) and bring to a boil. Reduce heat, and simmer until tender, about 1 hour, skimming as necessary. Remove meat, discard vegetables, and strain stock. Continue to boil stock until it's reduced to about 2 qt.

Place rice in a large saucepan or 10-cup rice cooker. Add 6 cups stock; reserve rest of stock. Bring rice to a boil. Then simmer for about 20 minutes.

Cook bacon until crisp, remove, and use it to snack on while you're making the rest of the boudin. Chop green onions, keeping white and green parts separate. Add green onion bottoms (white), onions, and garlic to drippings and sauté for a few minutes until onions are translucent.

Slice liver $^1/_2$ inch thick and add. Cook until liver is tender. Add about $^1/_2$ cup pork stock to pan, and cook for 10 more minutes, until most of the stock has reduced.

Put pork, liver, and vegetable mixture through a meat grinder with a course disc, or grind it coarse in a food processor. Transfer mixture to a large bowl and mix in green onions tops (green), 4 tbsp. minced parsley leaves, salt, peppers, and cooked rice. If it seems too dry, add more stock. It should be moist but not runny.

For traditional boudin, stuff mixture into sausage casings. Boudin links are generally about 1 foot long. You can also serve this without a casing as a rice dressing or main dish.

Serve freshly made or store in refrigerator. Heat in 350-degree oven for 10-15 minutes, until boudin is heated through and skin is crackly. Serve hot with crackers.

Chuck says, "If you want to try a fancy boudin presentation, try something that Café des Amis in Breaux Bridge does for an appetizer. Take 2 triangles of puff pastry, and place about $^1/_3$-$^1/_2$ cup boudin mixture on 1 pastry and cover with the other. Pinch around the edges until sealed. Make sure the edges don't leak. Brush the top with beaten egg and bake at 350 degrees until the pastry is puffed and golden brown. Drizzle with Louisiana cane syrup, some pepper jelly, and a little Creole mustard, and garnish the plate with finely diced red, green, and yellow bell peppers."

ANDOUILLE

Andouille (pronounced "ahn-DOO-wee") is the Cajun smoked sausage so famous nationally today. Made with pork butt or shank and pork fat, this sausage is seasoned with salt, cracked black pepper, and garlic. The andouille is then slowly smoked over pecan wood or sugarcane. When smoked, it becomes very dark to almost black in color. It is not uncommon for the Cajuns to smoke andouille for 7-8 hours at approximately 175 degrees.

True andouille is stuffed into beef middle casing, which makes the sausage approximately $1^1/_2$ inches in diameter. In parts of Germany, where some say andouille originated, the sausage was seasoned, made with all remaining intestine casings pulled through a larger casing, and smoked. It was served thinly sliced as an hors d'oeuvre. Traditionally, the andouilles from France were seasoned heavily, stuffed into the large intestines and stomach of the pig, and smoked. It is interesting to note that the finest andouille in France comes from Brittany and Normandy. It is believed that over half of the Acadian exiles who came to Louisiana in 1755 were originally from these coastal regions.

CHEF JOHN FOLSE'S ANDOUILLE
from Louisiana's Premier Products, Gonzales, LA

5 lb. pork butt
$^1/_2$ lb. pork fat
$^1/_2$ c. chopped garlic
$^1/_4$ c. cracked black pepper
2 Tbsp. cayenne pepper
1 Tbsp. dry thyme
4 Tbsp. salt
6 feet beef middle casing (see butcher or specialty shop)

Cooking with Crazy Charley IV

Cut pork butt into 1½-inch cubes. Using a meat grinder with four ¼-inch holes in the grinding plate, grind pork and pork fat. If you do not have a grinding plate this size, I suggest hand cutting pork butt into ¼-inch square pieces.

Place ground pork in a large mixing bowl and blend in seasonings. Once well blended, stuff meat into casings in 1-foot links, using the sausage attachment on your meat grinder. Tie both ends of each sausage securely using a heavy gauge twine.

In your home-style smoker, smoke andouille at 175-200 degrees for approximately 4-5 hours using pecan or hickory wood. Andouille may then be frozen and used for seasoning gumbos, white or red beans, or pastas or grilling as an hors d'oeuvre.

TASSO
from Chef Alex Patout

Tasso, a highly seasoned, intensely flavored smoked pork, adds a wonderful flavor to a variety of dishes, from soups and jambalayas to pastas and seafood dishes. It is easily obtainable in Louisiana or by mail order (see "Resources" chapter) but fun to make yourself. Here is Chef Alex Patout's recipe. (His restaurant is at 221 Royal Street in New Orleans.)

8 to 10 lb. boneless pork butt
5 Tbsp. salt
5 Tbsp. cayenne pepper
3 Tbsp. freshly ground black pepper
3 Tbsp. white pepper
2 Tbsp. paprika
2 Tbsp. cinnamon
2 Tbsp. garlic powder

Trim pork of all excess fat and cut pork into strips about 1 inch thick and at least 4 inches long. Mix seasonings together and place in a shallow pan. Roll each strip of pork in seasonings and place on a tray. Cover tray with plastic wrap and refrigerate at least overnight (preferably a couple of days).

Prepare your smoker. Place pork strips on a grill or rod and smoke until done, 5-7 hours. Don't let smoker get too hot.

Remove meat and let cool completely. Then wrap well in plastic and foil.

The tasso will keep well in the refrigerator for up to 10 days, and it also freezes very well.

MORE ON SAUSAGES AND OUR FAVORITE SAUSAGE MAKERS

My mother used to make sausage for our family. She used ground pork and just added rubbed sage, salt, and pepper to taste. It doesn't get simpler than that. It was a great breakfast sausage and easy to make. You can make sausage at home by adding spices and herbs that bring pleasure to your taste buds. I often use ground turkey in my mother's basic recipe and add herbs and spices. Sausage is best when made with meats that have fat to moisten them. When using turkey or chicken, you must either add fat or fillers such as breadcrumbs, egg, and moisture (water, broth, or milk).

Chef Paul Prudhomme's Cajun Magic is a good way to spice up meats and vegetables. He has blended spices together that complement beef, pork, poultry, or vegetables. Blended spices take the guesswork out of which spices to use where, and they keep your spice rack supplied with fewer and fresher spices and herbs. Paul suggests you add up the quantity of spices and herbs a recipe calls for, then add two-thirds of that amount of the appropriate Cajun Magic Spice. Check out Chef Paul Prudhomme's Web site (chefpaul.com.) to learn more about his many culinary awards, cookbooks, and Cajun Magic Spices.

Jimmy Dean, entertainer and investor in a pig ranch back in the mid-1960s, was eating sausage and eggs at a restaurant with his brother one morning. He was talking about the recent decline in the price of pork and the losses he was taking on his pig farm investment. Pulling out a large piece of gristle, he said, "Looks like someone could make a quality sausage." He got busy researching, testing, and tasting until he had a quality sausage, and he started his own business making sausage from pork. His business became successful and there are now over 40 products using his brand name. Read Jimmy Dean's autobiography, published in 2004. It's very interesting.

Chef Bruce Aidells owned a restaurant in Berkeley, California, where he started making sausages in 1983. He felt there was a need for a leaner sausage. He is a master chef who now markets his sausages made from chicken and turkey with fruits and vegetables. He has authored 10 cookbooks and writes for food magazines. Read about him on his Web site (aidells.com), and get his recipes for making sausage.

Following are a couple of recipes you can use to make your own sausage. Fresh sausage is the easiest to make, but if you really want to experience sausage making at home, you can buy through the Internet all the equipment you need to grind meats, stuff meats, and dry or smoke your homemade sausages. For everything you need to make sausage at home, go to sausagemaker.com. It has a catalog that includes a sausage cookbook with over 190 recipes. Or check out the Web for more sausage-making equipment and supplies.

RABBIT SAUSAGE BUSINESS

Several years ago, my cousin Pauline's husband, Udell, ran a feed store. One day, an old customer, named Homer, came to get some supplies. Udell asked him how his rabbit sausage business was doing.

Homer said that it was doing so well that he had trouble supplying his customers. Udell asked what he did to meet the demand for his rabbit sausage. Homer said that he would mix in a little mule to stretch the rabbit meat.

Little Tejon was standing by listening to this conversation. He spoke up and said that was what his daddy did too. Homer turned to Tejon and asked how much mule he used in his rabbit sausage. Little Tejon said about half and half, one rabbit to one mule.

BASIC PORK SAUSAGE

---

1 lb. ground pork
1-2 Tbsp. sage
$^1/_2$ tsp. each salt and black pepper
OR 1 tsp. Cajun Powder or good Cajun seasoning

Mix ingredients until well blended. Wrap in plastic wrap or place in airtight bowl and refrigerate for 12 to 24 hours to let flavors marry.

Form sausage patties and broil or fry. Broil by arranging on a wire rack and placing 5 inches under broiler, broiling slowly for 8-10 minutes, turning several times. Pan fry sausages in medium-hot skillet until brown, turn, and cook on other side. Pork is the most popular meat for sausage making because of its fat content and flavor.

Add your favorite spice or herb to this recipe, such as fresh minced garlic or garlic powder, onion powder, dry mustard, white pepper, ground ginger, chopped fresh parsley, dried thyme, or crushed dried red pepper flakes. Pork has fat to keep it moist so it needs no oils, eggs, or breadcrumbs to keep it from being dry.

GROUND TURKEY SAUSAGE

1 $1/2$ lb. ground turkey
2 Tbsp. dried breadcrumbs
1 egg, lightly beaten
2 cloves garlic, minced
2 tsp. sage
$1/2$ tsp. dried thyme
$1/2$ tsp. dried marjoram
$1/2$ tsp. salt
$1/2$ tsp. ground black pepper
$1/2$ tsp. cayenne pepper or Cajun Powder

Mix all ingredients in a bowl and stir until well mixed. Refrigerate for at least 1 hour to let spices marry. Use for breakfast patties; make them 2-3 inches in diameter and fry in 2 Tbsp. vegetable or olive oil. Brown in skillet on both side, then simmer until done. Use this sausage recipe for casseroles, with scrambled eggs, or in a meatloaf.

SAUSAGE SPOON BREAD
from Jenny Beadsley

Use the basic pork sausage recipe for this delicious spoon bread. Crumble the bulk sausage into a medium-hot cast-iron skillet. Cook until brown (drain most of the fat to lower calories).

Pour corn bread batter over sausage and bake in skillet until corn bread is done (use your favorite corn bread recipe or the recipe for Southern corn bread in this book). Cool slightly and turn out upside down on platter. Cut into slices and serve with eggs for breakfast or soup for lunch.

CAJUN EGGS

I met the fascinating master chef Joe Eiden, who serves Sicilian gumbo and other delightful Louisiana dishes in his Papa Joe's Kitchen restaurants in Reno and Los Angeles. His maternal grandfather left Sicily, ended up in New Orleans, and fell in love with the food and a Louisiana girl. Young Joe learned to love his grandfather's Louisiana/Sicilian cooking. Young Joe worked with Chef John Folse and Paul Prudhomme before opening his restaurants. The following recipe is an example of what can be found on his menu.

6 eggs
3 Tbsp. butter
$^1/_2$ lb. ground mild sausage
1 green bell pepper, diced
1 small red onion, diced
2 tsp. Cajun Powder
Tabasco sauce to taste
Mixed grated cheeses
4 pita breads, halved

Crack eggs into a bowl. Whip until they can't take it anymore! Now take a skillet big enough to hold everything. Add butter, then sausage. When it is pretty well cooked, add pepper and onion, and sauté till tender. Then add eggs. Cook and scramble.

Add Cajun Powder and Tabasco. Top with cheese. Turn off skillet and don't burn eggs. Put all this into bread halves and serve hot. Add more Tabasco if needed.

CAJUN CHILI WITH SAUSAGE

This is Charley's own recipe. Remember, good chili should not be too mild but not so hot that the heat interferes with the flavor. You can substitute another spicy BBQ sauce for my "great" hot Cajun sauce if mine is not available. This is the best chili recipe I have ever known, I guarantee! I gave this recipe and some of my hot Cajun sauce to the Budweiser distributor in our area. Budweiser was sponsoring a chili contest. Three weeks later, six cases of Bud were in my office doorway when I arrived at work. My recipe had won first place. It has also won several local contests. Now it's your turn, so make some!

2 c. beef broth
1 8-oz. can tomato sauce
1 15-oz. can stewed tomatoes
$^1/_2$ c. Crazy Charley Cajun sauce (original or hot)

2¹/₂ Tbsp. Jalapeno Pouring Sauce
1 medium onion, chopped
Salt to taste
¹/₄ c. olive oil
8 oz. Basic Pork Sausage
3-4 lb. tri-tip or sirloin of beef, cut into ¹/₂-inch chunks
4-8 Tbsp. quality chili powder (to taste)
2 tsp. Worcestershire sauce
2 tsp. garlic powder or fresh minced garlic
1 Tbsp. cumin
6 oz. beer

Spray bottom and sides of an 8-qt. deep pot or Dutch oven with nonstick spray. Place pot on medium heat. Add broth, tomato sauce, stewed tomatoes, Cajun sauce, jalapeno sauce, onion, and salt, and stir.

In a large (I prefer cast-iron) skillet, add half the olive oil, and crumble sausage into skillet. Cook over medium-high heat until browned. Dump into pot. Brown beef cubes in remaining olive oil, in 2 batches if needed. Sprinkle with 1 Tbsp. chili powder and the Worcestershire sauce and cook until brown. Dump browned beef into pot and stir to blend.

Stir into pot the garlic, cumin, salt to taste, remaining chili powder, and beer. Bring to a boil, cover pot with a lid, lower heat, and simmer for 1 hour 40 minutes, stirring every 20-30 minutes. After simmering, taste and add more Cajun sauce or jalapeno sauce to taste.

Keep the cover off and simmer for an additional 30-40 minutes to let it thicken, stirring occasionally.

WOW! Eat over rice. Serve with potato salad and Southern Corn Bread. Serves 20 of your friends and/or family.

"I'D LIKE SOME CAJUN SAUSAGE"

A guy goes into a store and tells the clerk, "I'd like some Cajun sausage." The clerk looks at him and asks, "Are you Cajun?" The guy, clearly offended, says, "Well, yes, I am. But let me ask you something. If I had asked for Italian sausage, would you ask me if I was Italian? Or if I had asked for German sausage, would you ask me if I was German? Or if I asked for Jewish sausage, would you ask me if I was Jewish? Or if I had asked for a taco, would you ask if I was Mexican? Huh? Would ya?"

The clerk says, "Well, no." With deep self-righteous indignation, the guy says, "Well, all right then. Why did you ask me if I'm Cajun just because I ask for Cajun sausage."

"Because this is a hardware store."

MENU PLANNING AND RECIPES

MENU PLANNING
by Ruth

Many of the recipes in this book have suggestions for what to serve with it to complete the meal.

When planning the different courses for your meals, remember good food appeals to all the senses, not just taste. Use foods that will stimulate visual pleasure, foods that represent various colors. If you are serving a white meat such as chicken or pork, serve yams or sweet potatoes, a green vegetable, and/or garden salad. Serve a light dessert with a complex main course.

Never underestimate the sense of smell when it comes to enticing your diners. Our olfactory system or sense of smell can detect hundreds of scents. Everyone reacts in a personal way to all scents. We have a friend who enjoys the smell of a skunk. Researchers gave migraine sufferers tubes that released the smell of green apples. Most of them reported their headache pain was relieved. The smell brought no relief to those who disliked the smell of apples or who had a reduced sense of smell. Food aromas can stimulate appetites, remind of previous eating experiences, tells you if food is spoiled, or cause allergies to act up, or make you sick. Include compatibility of the aroma of each food being prepared in meal planning.

Many people enjoy food with texture and how the food feels in their mouth. A customer told me she didn't like chunky salsa. She was unable to find a smooth textured salsa with flavor she liked. Our piquante/salsa is chunky, but she liked the flavor. I suggested she put it in her blender and change its texture. She bought 2 jars and wondered why she hadn't thought of that. Plan a menu of dishes with various textures to please the palate and the sense of touch and feel.

Many cultures accept noisy food and noisy diners. In our melted culture, most people are annoyed with people who make noises when they eat. Smacking, slurping, gulping, banging silverware, such noises are not acceptable while eating. Crisp celery and carrot sticks, crackers, and chips may be an exception.

We compliment the cook on how wonderful a meal tastes. Our sense of taste is limited to sweet, sour, salty, spicy, and tart and varying degrees of each. Our sense of taste is stimulated by the foods we put into our mouth. Everyone has a unique set of taste buds and experience sweet, sour, salty, spicy, and tart differently. Study's show that some people have more taste buds than others. Through inherited traits, we can thank our ancestors for the degrees of rich and spicy or the mild flavors we enjoy. Good eating doesn't have to be painful nor does it have to be tasteless. Keep this in mind when planning your menu and know the preferences of your diners. There is no such thing as wimpy food or too spicy food. The goal of eating is to enjoy the flavor, aroma, vision, texture, and even the little noises food provides while nourishing our bodies in the process.

The following recipes are recipes enjoyed by Cajuns that do not call for Crazy Charley sauces. These recipes will help you complete your menu planning with bread, salads, vegetables, and dessert. Many come from Charles' family recipe box.

HUSHPUPPIES

    1$^1/_2$ c. corn meal
    $^1/_2$ c. flour
    1 Tbsp. baking powder
    1 tsp. Cajun powder (or 1 tsp. salt and pepper)
    $^1/_2$ tsp. dried parsley
    2 Tbsp. vegetable oil
    1 c. low fat milk
    2 eggs, beaten
    Oil for deep-frying (vegetable or peanut oil)

Mix all dry ingredients; add eggs and blend. Add milk and oil and mix well. Heat 3 to 4 inches vegetable oil to 350 degrees. Drop mixture by desired spoon size into hot oil. Cook until golden brown on each side or 1 minute per side. Drain on paper towel.

Lagniappe: Add $^1/_4$ cup finely chopped green onions and/or 1 teaspoon minced garlic to batter and fresh oregano for parsley. For a treat add $^1/_2$ cup piquante/salsa.

                                        Cooking with Crazy Charley IV

SOUTHERN CORN BREAD

1$^1/_2$ c. yellow corn meal
$^1/_2$ c. flour
1 tsp. sugar
1 Tbsp. baking powder
1 tsp. salt
$^1/_4$ c. vegetable oil
1 large egg
1 cup milk

Preheat oven to 450 degrees. Mix dry ingredients in a medium sized mixing bowl until well blended. Beat vegetable oil, eggs, and milk in small bowl until frothy. Pour into dry ingredients and stir just until blended.

Place 1 tablespoon of vegetable oil in 8-9-inch cast iron or heavy oven-proof skillet over high heat on stovetop for 1-2 minutes. Pour batter into hot skillet; spread evenly with a spoon. Place in hot 400-degree oven. Bake 18-20 minutes or until it pulls away from the sides of the skillet and is brown. Serve hot from the oven. Serves 8.

Lagniappe: For variety, add $^3/_4$ cup of piquante/salsa or 1 cup canned creamed corn in place of $^1/_2$ cup of milk.

BUTTERMILK BISCUITS

2 cups flour
1 tsp. salt
1$^1/_2$ tsp. baking powder
$^1/_2$ tsp. baking soda
4 Tbsp. shortening
1 cup buttermilk

Mix dry ingredients; cut in shortening. Add buttermilk and mix. Knead lightly in small amount of flour. Roll $^1/_2$ to 1 inch thick. Cut in rounds with floured cutter. Place on greased baking sheet in very hot 450-degree oven for 12 to 15 minutes, until brown, makes 9 to 12 biscuits. Charles made these biscuits and Ruth made sausage red eye gravy for two years at a breakfast following early morning bird watching at a festival. YUM!

SWEET POTATO BISCUITS

1 1/2 cups flour
2 Tbsp. baking powder
3/4 tsp. salt
1/2 cup shortening
1 cup milk
1 1/2 cups mashed sweet potatoes (I use Bruce brand canned yams)

Sift dry ingredients; cut in shortening. Mix milk with sweet potatoes and add to first mixture. Knead lightly in small amount of flour; roll to 1/2-inch thick. Cut with floured cutter. Put on greased sheet and bake at 425 degrees for 12 to 15 minutes. Makes 15 to 20 biscuits.

GREENS SOUTHERN STYLE

2 bunches turnip, mustard, or collard greens
1/4 lb. salt pork, cut into 4 pieces
1 tsp. salt
1 tsp. sugar

Wash greens and strip leaves from stalk. Fill a 6quart pot 1/2 full of water. Place greens in pot; add salt, sugar, and pork. Bring to boil; simmer for 2 hours. Watch the water level so pot keeps enough water to make pot liquor. Serve as a side dish or main dish with hot pepper sauce (hot peppers soaked in vinegar) and a slice of Bermuda (or sweet) onions. Serves 6.

Lagniappe: To lower the fat, substitute beef bouillon for the salt pork. Charley saves the pot liquor (liquid greens are cooked in). The next day, he adds crumbled leftover corn bread to the pot liquor and has visions of being in heaven as he eats it. That's sopping!

Cajuns add a little sugar to vegetables. It enhances the flavor much like MSG.

BLACK-EYED PEAS AND OKRA

2 cups black-eyed peas (fresh, canned, or frozen)*
1 lb. okra (fresh, canned, or frozen)**
1/4 lb. salt pork, cut into pieces
1 1/2 tsp. Cajun powder or salt and pepper

When using canned peas and okra, sauté salt pork in skillet until cooked. Add to canned peas, okra, and seasonings. Eliminate all or part of the fat, if desired, and simmer for 10 minutes.

When using fresh or frozen peas and okra, cook black-eyed peas as directed on package or for 60 minutes with salt pork and seasonings. Add the fresh or frozen okra after peas have cooked for 30 minutes and simmer until peas are tender. Serves 6 to 8.

*Substitute field peas or crowder peas.

**Studies show canned vegetables to be as nutritious as frozen and maybe more than fresh, depending on the length of time fresh vegetables have been harvested. Vegetables are canned and frozen within 12 hours of harvest. Vegetables begin to lose nutrients as soon as they are picked.

CHILI MAQUE CHOUX

1 to 2 Tbsp. olive oil
2 cups frozen, fresh, or canned whole kernel corn
1 (15 oz.) can white hominy (optional)
1 cup julienne onions
$^1/_2$ cup julienne green bell pepper
1 tsp. Cajun Powder or salt and pepper
1 heaping tsp. quality chili powder
1 tsp. brown sugar
$^1/_2$ cup evaporated milk (or chicken broth for dairy free)

In 1 quart saucepan, heat oil; add corn, onions, peppers, chili, and seasoning. Cook over medium heat for 5 minutes, stirring frequently. Add sugar, hominy, and milk and simmer 5 minutes. Serve as a side dish with grilled meats and fish or with seafood jambalaya. Serves 4 to 6.

Lagniappe: Add 1 pound of shrimp and omit the hominy and chili for a main dish. Serves 4.

LOUISIANA CAKE

$^1/_2$ cup light sour cream
1 c. sugar*
2 eggs
Dash of salt
2 cups flour*
1 tsp. baking soda
1 cup crushed pineapple

Place sour cream, sugar, and eggs in large mixing bowl and beat until frothy. In another bowl, blend flour and baking soda and add to sour cream mixture. Beat well, at least 50 strokes. Fold in pineapple and $^1/_2$ cup of finely chopped pecans. Pour into lightly oiled tube pan. Bake in pre-heated 350-degree oven for 35 minutes, until done. Glaze with Coconut Pecan Icing.

Icing:

4-8 oz. cream cheese
2 Tbsp. shredded coconut
1 tsp. vanilla
1 cup powdered sugar
4 Tbsp. finely chopped pecans

Combine ingredients and stir until smooth. Pour or spread over cake when cooled. Makes 12 servings.

*This cake is great for diabetics—use sugar substitute and whole-grain flour such as old-fashioned oats (put oatmeal in a blender to make oat flour), rye, or whole wheat in place of half the flour. For icing use light cream cheese, 2 Tbsp. sugar substitute, and chopped pecans.

PECAN PIE

Since we are concentrating on the land that time forgot and good eating is king, here is Charley's mother's recipe for Pecan Pie.

$^1/_2$ cup sugar
3 large or 4 small eggs
Dash of salt

1 cup dark corn syrup or molasses
1 stick ($^1/_4$ lb.) butter
$1^1/_2$ cups coarsely chopped pecans
1 tsp. vanilla

Preheat oven to 450 degrees. Cream sugar and butter, add eggs, 1 at a time, mixing thoroughly after each egg is added; do not over beat. Add the remaining ingredients and mix lightly. Pour into a 9-inch pie shell. Bake for 10 minutes. Reduce heat to 350 degrees and bake 30 minutes more. Let the pie cool. Serve cold or at room temperature. Serves 8.

Lagniappe: Arrange pecan halves around the outer edge of pie before baking.

OATMEAL CAKE

1 c. quick oatmeal
1 1/2 c. boiling water
1 cube (1/4 lb.) margarine or butter

Mix; let stand 20 minutes.

$1^1/_2$ c. flour
$^3/_4$ c. brown sugar
$^1/_2$ c. granulated sugar
1 tsp. soda
1 tsp. baking powder
$^1/_2$ tsp. salt
1 tsp. cinnamon
$^1/_2$ tsp. nutmeg
2 eggs

Combine dry ingredients until blended. Beat eggs; stir into oatmeal mixture. Add flour mixture in 3 parts, mixing well with each addition. Pour into lightly greased 9x13 inch baking pan. Bake in preheated 350-degree oven for 30 minutes or until done. Glaze with icing as soon as cake is removed from oven.

Icing Glaze:

4 Tbsp. light cream cheese
$^1/_2$ c. powdered sugar
$^1/_4$ c. brown sugar
$^1/_4$ c. chopped pecans
$^1/_4$ c. shredded coconut
3 Tbsp. milk

Mix until smooth. Spread over hot cake. Serve warm.

PECAN BREAD PUDDING

6 slices buttered sweet French bread
$^1/_2$ c. chopped pecans
2 eggs
$^1/_4$ tsp. salt
2 c. milk
$^1/_2$ c. sugar
1 tsp. vanilla

Cut buttered bread into 1 inch squares. Arrange in layers in buttered baking dish. Sprinkle each layer with pecans. Beat eggs lightly; add sugar, salt, vanilla, and milk. Mix well; pour over bread. Garnish top with pecans. Bake at 325 degrees for 1 hour. Serves 4 to 6.

Pecan Sauce:

1 c. sugar
$^1/_2$ c. condensed milk
2 Tbsp. corn syrup

Combine in 2 quart saucepan. Cook until it forms softball in cold water. Remove from heat.

Add:

$^3/_4$ c. chopped pecans
4 Tbsp. butter
$^1/_2$ tsp. vanilla

Beat until butter melts. Pour over bread pudding. Serve warm.

For a praline sauce, substitute $^1/_2$ cup brown sugar for granulated sugar and follow the rest of the recipe.

This makes a great topping for ice cream, bread pudding, or the Oatmeal Cake.

CHARLEY'S FAVORITE OLD RECIPES FROM FAMILY, FRIENDS, AND RESTAURANTS

Folks, all of these recipes are tried and true. None of them are new, in fact, most are over 100 years old. One of my "Cookbook" references is "La Cuisine Creole" published in 1885! Many are begged, borrowed, or cajoled from some of South Louisiana's best restaurants and cafes. Others are taken from my family archives. Several recipes come from my brother-in-law, Julius Champagne's family. One thing for sure, you are going to love every one; you hear!

BON APPETIT, Y'ALL.

THE ROUX (ROO)

When you hear the term "roux" in south Louisiana, they are not referring to kangaroos, but to a cooking mixture that is used to flavor and give color and texture.

Paul Prudhomme told me one time that the roux goes so far back in history that its origin cannot be traced.

In the old days it was a mixture of animal fat and flour cooked very slowly in an iron skillet or pot for a very long time. Paul has a method of cooking the roux on a high heat for a short period of time. I tend to use the old way, the way I was taught, slow and easy. I was taught to make two roux's: The first and more traditional roux with flour and oil in equal parts: the second with tomato paste and a smaller amount of oil. To those of us watching calories and fat, this is the best one and it can be used in nearly all recipes that call for a Roux. In my recipes, I will state if either Roux, one or two, should be used. If I don't mention a specific Roux, either may be used.

ROUX NO. 1 (TRADITIONAL)

$^3/_4$ **cup all-purpose flour (not self-rising flour)**
$^3/_4$ **cup good cooking oil**

In a clean, heavy skillet or a two-quart saucepan (not aluminum), stir the flour and oil together until it's well blended. Cook on medium-high for 10 minutes. Reduce the heat to just below medium or medium-low. Simmer about 45 minutes, stirring often. The roux should be consistent

135

in texture. This will give you a rich, dark brown roux. If lighter roux is required, cook 15 minutes less. The roux can be cooked and stored in refrigerator for several months. For this reason, I usually make a quart of roux and store it for use as needed.

ROUX NO. 2

2 (6 oz.) cans tomato paste or 1 (12 oz.) can
6 oz. cooking oil (not olive oil)

Just like the first, mix together in clean skillet or pot; cook the same way except cook for entire 45 minutes and stir, stir, stir. (Note: Don't let roux stick to pan.) This roux also can be stored.

There you have it, folks, one of the secrets of Creole and Cajun food.

THE ART OF FRYING
by Charley

Frying fish, chicken, rabbit, squirrels, quail, dove, alligator, eel, shrimp, frog legs, okra, green tomatoes, hush puppies, and dill pickles is just our way of life. I still believe there is nothing in this world better than a platter of fried channel cat. Serve with hush puppies and Cole slaw, of course.

When I was growing up, everything was fried in lard (pig fat) and all the grease from frying bacon was hoarded as the best flavor ingredient available. I don't seem to remember anyone warning about saturated fat or cholesterol.

Now I am not suggesting you start using lard for your frying, but knowing how to fry food properly will make it delicious and with a minimum of absorbed fat. I now use a cholesterol-free corn oil to do my frying in. Do not use olive oil for frying because it burns at a lower temperature than vegetable oil.

The batter used in frying is critical. I am going to give you the recipe for a couple of batters we use.

BEER BATTER FOR FISH
OR ANYTHING WORTH FRYING

$^3/_4$ cup Bisquick or equivalent
$^1/_3$ cup warm beer
1 tsp. oil

2 egg whites, beaten stiff
1 tsp. salt
1 tsp. black pepper
$^1/_2$ tsp. garlic powder

Mix together well. Dip fish into batter and fry in hot oil until brown. Turn often and drain on paper towels or brown paper bag.

Folks, this batter is great for frying carrots, broccoli, and celery in. Try it, y'all.

GOOD OLD SOUTHERN BATTER

Friends, I know that frying has lately gotten a bad reputation, but I think most of it is undeserved. This is a good old southern batter that is great for frog legs, seafood, or anything you just want to fry.

1 c. flour
2 Tbsp. cornstarch
1 tsp. salt
1 Tbsp. baking powder
2 eggs
1 c. cold water

Mix flour, cornstarch, salt, and baking powder in bowl. Add whole eggs and mix well into a batter that is smooth. Add cold water and continue to mix until batter is quite thin and smooth.

RANDOL'S HUSH PUPPIES

Folks, there is nothing as good or as necessary to a seafood feast as "Hush Puppies." Here is the recipe from The Cajun Restaurant, Randol's of Lafayette.

1 c. yellow corn meal
1 c. all-purpose flour
2 tsp. baking powder
$^1/_4$ tsp. baking soda
$^1/_2$ c. sugar
$^1/_2$ tsp. salt
1 egg
$^1/_2$ cup buttermilk

Heat approximately 3 inches pure vegetable oil to 350 degrees in deep heavy pot.

Meanwhile, in large bowl with fork, mix corn meal, flour, baking powder, sugar, salt, and baking soda. In small bowl with fork, beat egg and buttermilk until thoroughly blended. Slowly stir egg mixture into cornmeal mixture forming smooth batter. (Batter should be thick; additional cornmeal may be added if necessary.) Using a 2-ounce ice cream scoop, drop balls into hot oil, a few at a time, and fry until golden brown. Drain on paper toweling. Serve piping hot with butter, or any favorite jam or preserves. Makes 16.

RANDOL'S CAJUN BARBEQUE SHRIMP

A Cajun shrimp scampi, if you will.

Mix seasoning together:

    1 tsp. salt
    $^1/_4$ tsp. garlic
    $^1/_4$ tsp. onion powder
    $^1/_8$ tsp. thyme
    $^1/_8$ tsp. paprika
    $^1/_8$ tsp. oregano
    $^1/_4$ tsp. black pepper
    Dash of white pepper
    Dash of red pepper

Measure 1 tablespoon of above seasoning, add 1 tablespoon black pepper and $^1/_2$ teaspoon rosemary. This completes the seasoning mix.

    $^1/_4$ lb. butter
    1 Tbsp. fresh garlic
    1 Tbsp. seasoning mix (from above)
    4 oz. beer
    2 oz. Worcestershire sauce
    2 lb. large shrimp in shells

In a saucepan, sauté shrimp with shell on in butter. Add garlic, seasoning, beer, and Worcestershire sauce and simmer over medium heat for 5 minutes.

BOILING SHELLFISH
by Charley

One of my greatest disappointments as far as food is concerned was eating crab and shrimp at the famous San Francisco Fisherman's Wharf. I had been looking forward to dining on great seafood at the famous spot.

Well, I couldn't believe that they didn't even season the water they cooked the crustaceans in. They just boiled them in water with salt. Shellfish need to be boiled in seasoned water. To get the best flavor from shellfish, follow these simple directions.

This recipe is for 2 pounds of shrimp or crawfish.

Fill a large stockpot, at least eight quarts, a little more than half full of cold water.

Add the following to the pot:

  1 c. chopped celery
  3 chopped green onions
  Juice of whole lemon
  3 Tbsp. salt
  Bag of crab or shrimp boil or powdered crab boil

Crab or shrimp boil is a combination of herbs and spices sealed in a small porous bag. I like Zatarain's and Cajun Land the best. They can be purchased in specialty stores. If you can't find a boil ready-made, you can make your own by mixing together and putting mixture in an old-fashioned tea ball or in cheesecloth or grind in coffee grinder.

  $^1/_2$ tsp. coriander
  $^1/_2$ tsp. allspice
  $^1/_2$ tsp. mustard seed
  $^1/_2$ tsp. cayenne pepper
  $^1/_2$ tsp. black pepper
  1 bay leaves, chopped

Bring water and seasoning to boil; cover and simmer for 20 minutes, letting the full flavor of the seasonings mix with the water. Turn off heat and let flavors marry for about 10 more minutes.

Bring mixture back to rapid boil. Dump shrimp or crawfish into water and turn heat off and let stand for 6 to 8 minutes. Boy, oh boy, you have great tasting shrimp or crawfish. I guarantee!

For crab and lobster, boil 5 minutes after putting them into water. Turn off heat and follow instructions in previous paragraph.

One of the most frequent questions I get asked is, "why are my shrimp gritty when I serve them?" Well, folks, shrimp have a vein that runs down their backs and on all shrimp of any size one must remove the vein, sweetheart, before eating.

SEAFOOD BAKED POTATO

Friends, this dish is always on "special" at Dave's Cajun Kitchen in Houma, Louisiana. You can use it as an entree or a side dish. It's great, you hear!

1 potato per person (I am using 2 potatoes for this recipe)
2 oz. butter or margarine
2 oz. crabmeat (canned crabmeat will do)
2 oz. cooked shrimp, small to medium, deveined
2 oz. sour cream
2 oz. Cheddar cheese

Bake potatoes in a 350-degree oven for 1 hour. You may microwave them if you wish. Remove baked potatoes and wrap in aluminum foil. Split the potatoes in half. Add $^1/_2$ of each ingredient to each potato. Return to hot oven or microwave and bake until the cheese is all melted. Serves 2.

CRAWFISH
by Charley

We are talking about that wonderful, delectable "mud bug" named Crawfish. They are not called "Crayfish." That's outlander talk. It's Crawfish all the way, you hear!

These tasty miniature lobsters have a sweetness even shrimp don't possess. Crawfish should be boiled in salty water using a good crab, shrimp, and crawfish boil. They must be alive when boiled. If their tails are curled under after boiling, then you know they were cooked while alive. Do not eat ones with a straight tail as it probably was already dead before it was cooked. These shellfish should be dumped into boiling, seasoned, and salty water. Return to boil and turn off heat. Let crawfish seep for 5 minutes; pour into colander and get ready to really enjoy these "Louisiana Lobsters."

The meat is in the tail and they are small, so you should cook a pound per person. To eat, pick up the crustacean between thumb and forefinger. Gently twist tail away from the head. Pull off the first several sections of shell at large end of the tail. Hold the small end of tail and pull out the meat from the large end. You may use Felix's cocktail sauce, if you so desire, but they are morsels fit for a king without any condiment added. We then suck the wonderful juice from the head.

Cajuns don't waste any part of the "mud bug," I guarantee.

Now you understand what the old Cajun saying "pinch the tails and suck the heads" means.

You will love these delectable creatures and will develop a craving for them from time to time, just like a good Cajun.

MADEWOOD PLANTATION'S CRAWFISH ETOUFEE

1 c. flour
3 Tbsp. cooking oil
$^1/_2$ c. chopped onion
$^1/_2$ c. chopped green bell pepper
1 can chicken broth
$^1/_3$ c. vermouth or fine wine
1 lb. crawfish tails (or shrimp, chicken, or sausage)
Salt and pepper to taste
Tabasco sauce to taste (optional)
3 c. cooked rice

Brown flour and 1 Tbsp. oil to make a roux. In separate pan, sauté vegetables in remaining oil and add to roux. Add broth and wine, mix well, then add crawfish. Add salt and pepper (and Tabasco if desired). Cook over low heat about $1^1/_2$ hours until crawfish is tender. Serve over rice. Serves 5.

CORNBREAD

I remarked before that cornbread was the first thing my grandmother Oliver taught me to cook. I was nine years old. This staple should not be hard to bake. I have had more lousy cornbread than anything else I can think of.

Too many people think it should taste and have the consistency of cake. Can you imagine eating cake and black-eyed peas or cake and collard greens—ugh.

I don't like cornbread that is too sweet. Now I know some people, even some Cajuns who like sweet bread, but not me. I notice that most Yankee cornbread is sweet and looks more like cake than cornbread. Many recipes do call for sugar to be added as a major ingredient. This is not the way I was taught and most people from south Louisiana don't eat if that way. Now understand, we do use a little sugar to marry the flavors in many dishes. We add a little sugar to vegetables and all tomato based dishes. I even use a little in my cornbread, but only a tablespoon.

There are ways to eat cornbread besides as bread at a meals. One way is to serve the warm cornbread in cold milk, or as I prefer it, in a tall glass of buttermilk. We also crumble it up in the juice of turnip or collard greens and call it "pot licker." Any way you use it, it's great.

As we shall see later, cornbread is also a great base for many kind of stuffing and dressings.

PERFECT OLD-FASHIONED CORNBREAD*

2 c. yellow cornmeal
$^1/_2$ c. all-purpose flour
$1^1/_2$ tsp. baking powder
1 Tbsp. sugar (optional)
1 tsp. salt
1 c. whole milk or evaporated milk
2 eggs
$^1/_4$ c. shortening (Crisco) or vegetable oil

Mix dry ingredients together in large mixing bowl. Cut shortening into mixture if shortening is used. Otherwise, mix eggs, milk, and oil together. Pour into dry mixture and blend well, but do not beat.

Grease a 9 or 10 inch iron skillet or other appropriate greased heavy baking pan. Nonstick products like Pam may be used to grease the skillet.

Pour mixture into skillet and set over medium-high burner on top of stove for about 2 minutes.

Put skillet in preheated 415-degree oven. Bake 20 to 25 minutes or until golden brown.

You may use sour or buttermilk. Use $1^1/_2$ cups of sour or buttermilk; add $^3/_4$ teaspoon of baking soda and only 1 teaspoon baking powder. Muffin pans may also be used instead of a skillet.

*Charley's mama used to make crackling bread. He grew up eating it and thought you should all know that by adding a cup of diced cracklings (fried pork skins) to the cornbread mixture you, too, can experience heaven.

OYSTER DRESSING
from Charley's mama

We have the best tasting oysters in the world, I guarantee!

My favorite stuffing or dressing, whichever you want to call it, is oyster dressing. I now tender my mama's recipe for this heavenly stuffing.

> 1 c. casually chopped onions
> 1 stick butter or margarine
> $1^1/_2$ lb. or 8 cups chopped old French bread
> 2 qt. chicken or turkey stock
> 12 medium to large oysters or 1 pt., cut in halves
> 2 tsp. salt
> 1 Tbsp. poultry seasoning
> 1 tsp. black pepper
> 1 tsp. thyme

Sauté the onions in butter until soft. Add stock and seasonings and bring to simmer. Add cut up oysters; return mixture to simmer and simmer for 5 minutes. Place chopped breadcrumbs in large mixing bowl. Pour hot mixture over breadcrumbs and mix well. Stuff bird or empty into a greased baking pan or dish and bake at 350 degrees for about $1^1/_2$ hours.

Folks, if you like oysters, you will adore this dressing.

DELICIOUS CORNBREAD STUFFING-DRESSING

2 c. crumbled cornbread
1 tsp. black pepper
1 tsp. dried thyme
1 Tbsp. sage
1 tsp. salt
1 c. diced celery
1 c. chopped onions
2 eggs
2 c. chicken or turkey stock
$^1/_4$ lb. butter or margarine

Combine dry ingredients in large mixing bowl. In a skillet, melt butter or margarine and slowly sauté onions and celery. Add stock when onions and celery are soft. Mix well and pour into dry ingredients and mix slowly until dry mixture is good and moist.

Stuff the bird, spoon remainder of dressing into greased baking pan, bake at 350 degrees for about 30 to 40 minutes.

Note: You may add cooked chicken or turkey giblets to this stuffing. We usually leave out the liver. The grandkids say "yuck" when they see the liver.

ROASTED GOOSE

We wanted to have something special for Christmas dinner. We were talking about it when Pierre, a chef friend, visited. He suggested a goose. He gave us this recipe.

1 large goose
2 Tbsp. butter
3 ribs celery, minced
1 medium onion, chopped
1 carrot, diced
3 shallots, chopped
3 large cloves garlic, chopped

Poultry seasoning (tarragon, thyme)
1 heaping Tbsp. flour
1$^1/_2$ c. red wine
1$^1/_2$ c. chicken broth

Select a large goose from a reputable supplier. Wash and prepare it for cooking. Brown the goose in a medium-hot skillet to remove fat.

Place butter in skillet and sauté vegetables and herbs. Sprinkle flour over vegetables and mix well. Add wine and stir until mixture thickens. Add broth and simmer for 5 minutes.

Place goose in roasting pan or Dutch oven and pour vegetable mixture over it. Do not cover with more than 2 inches of sauce. Roast according to weight of goose.

Serve with cabbage that is sautéed until just brown with onion, garlic, and cumin. Add desired amount of white wine or chicken broth to cabbage to moisten. Season cabbage with white vinegar and serve. Turnips, potatoes, or rice also make great side dishes, along with a fresh apple salad (recipe in this book).

SENATOR RUSSELL'S SWEET-POTATO CASSEROLE

3-4 c. mashed cooked sweet potatoes (canned is fine)
1 c. sugar
2 eggs
1 tsp. vanilla
$^1/_2$ c. milk
$^1/_2$ c. melted butter
1 packed c. brown sugar
$^1/_3$ c. flour
$^1/_2$ -1 c. chopped pecans (I use 1 c.)
$^1/_3$ c. butter, softened

Combine potatoes, sugar, eggs, vanilla, milk, and melted butter and put in buttered casserole. Mix brown sugar, flour, pecans, and softened butter and spread across top of potatoes. Bake at 350 degrees for 30 minutes. I always cook this at Christmas. It is almost like a dessert.

MADEWOOD PUMPKIN-YAM LAFOURCHE

1 c. pumpkin
3 c. drained yams
3 medium apples, peeled, cored, and sliced
1 c. sugar
$^1/_2$ c. raisins
$^1/_2$ tsp. vanilla
$^1/_2$ tsp. cinnamon
$^1/_2$ tsp. nutmeg
$^1/_2$ stick butter

Mix pumpkin and yams until smooth. Add apples, sugar, raisins, vanilla, cinnamon, and nutmeg; mix until well blended. Melt butter and mix in thoroughly. Bake at 150 degrees for about 30 minutes.

NEW ORLEANS MUFFALETTA SANDWICH
from Kevin Joubert

The New Orleans muffaletta is a sandwich supposedly created at Central Grocery in the French Quarter. This is a very old little Italian grocery store that is a "must" visit for anyone going to New Orleans. Look for it on Decatur Street as you are leaving the Jackson Square area on the way to the French Market. (I also had one at Pat O'Brien's that was good.)

The secret to the muffaletta is twofold—good bread and olive salad. It also contains thinly sliced cheese and meats—mostly ham, with some salami and maybe a little pepperoni tossed in. The type of ham and cheese is, in my opinion, irrelevant and can be changed to fit your taste or mood...but you can't make a muffaletta without some good bread and olive salad. To make your own focaccia, search the Internet for recipes.

1 large loaf or 4 small loaves Italian bread (or 2 loaves focaccia)
Ham (cappicola, prosciutto, honey ham, whatever...)
Salami (hard, Genoa, mortadella, whatever...)
Pepperoni (optional)
Cheese (provolone, mozzarella, American, or any combination)
Olive salad

Slice bread like hamburger bun(s) (focaccia doesn't need to be sliced, because it's usually thin). Lightly toast. Add alternating layers of meat, cheese, and olive salad to bottom bread slice (or top of focaccia). Pop this portion in oven to melt cheese. Put the whole thing together like a sandwich to enjoy. If using 1 large loaf, cut into quarters to serve.

MUFFALETTA

Many of you have asked for a good recipe for a muffaletta that includes homemade olive salad. This recipe is from Karen Stone and was published in the cookbook *The Top 100 New Orleans Recipes of All Time*, compiled by John DeMers and Rhonda Findley. This sandwich is popular in New Orleans.

1 c. chopped green olives with pimentos
$^3/_4$ c. chopped black olives in oil
$^1/_2$ c. olive oil
1 Tbsp. fresh oregano (or $^1/_2$ c. dried)
6 Tbsp. chopped fresh parsley
Salt and pepper to taste
2 tsp. minced garlic
1 tsp. fresh lemon juice
1 loaf round Italian bread
$^1/_4$ head iceberg lettuce, shredded
1 medium tomato, thinly sliced
$^1/_4$ lb. mortadella (sweet salami)
$^1/_4$ lb. sliced ham
$^1/_4$ lb. sliced mozzarella
$^1/_4$ lb. thinly sliced pepperoni

In a large mixing bowl, combine olives, oil, herbs, seasonings, garlic, and lemon juice. Cover and marinate overnight in refrigerator.

Cut Italian loaf in half to make a top and bottom, and hollow out bottom layer for filling.

Remove salad from refrigerator and drain. Divide salad in half. Place one-half on hollowed-out half of bread.

Layer with lettuce, tomato, meats, and cheese as listed. Top with remaining salad and place remaining bread on top. Wrap in plastic tightly and place on baking sheet. Top with a pan and weight down with heavy cans of food or a phonebook, etc.

Refrigerate a few hours. Flavors will meld and sandwich will be easier to slice. Cut sandwich in small pie-shaped slices and serve.

APPLE SALAD

1 head romaine lettuce
3 medium apples
1 c. diced celery
$^1/_2$ c. dried cranberries or raisins or a mixture
1 c. coarsely chopped walnuts
$^1/_2$ c. mayonnaise
$^1/_4$ c. milk
1 Tbsp. sugar
Pinch salt

Chop lettuce in small pieces. Wash and dry apples and cut in $^1/_2$-inch chunks. (My favorite apples for this salad are red or golden delicious or any sweet crunchy apple. Red apples add color and the peel works well in this salad, but apples can be peeled.) Toss lettuce, apples, celery, berries, and nuts together until mixed. Beat mayonnaise, milk, sugar, and salt until smooth and creamy, and toss with salad. Serves 6-8.

Note: When serving this for my grandchildren, I add 1 c. miniature marshmallows.

PRALINES

1 c. sugar
1 c. brown sugar
$^1/_2$ tsp. salt
1 c. canned milk (not sweetened condensed)
1 stick ($^1/_2$ cup) butter
1 tsp. vanilla
1 c. pecan halves

Combine sugars, salt, and milk. Stir over low heat until sugars dissolve. Stir constantly so mixture does not burn. Cook about 15 minutes to "soft ball" stage. Cool slightly.

Add butter, vanilla, and pecans (pronounced peh-KAN or puh-KON, not PEE-kan, the thing Grandmother kept under her bed). Beat until creamy. Drop by spoonfuls onto a piece of waxed paper and let harden. Makes 30-36 pralines.

For a great ice-cream topper, boil about 10 minutes. Do not let it form a ball in cold water. Serve warm over ice cream or pound cake. Thin it with milk if it gets too hard.

CAJUN COFFEE COOKIES

These are great! Cajuns use coffee in everything; it's our national beverage.

2 sticks unsalted butter, softened
$1^1/_4$ c. sugar
3 egg yolks
3 Tbsp. vanilla
$^1/_2$ c. good instant coffee powder (not liquid)
3 c. cake flour or well-sifted flour

Cream butter and sugar with mixer on high speed and set aside. In another bowl, place egg yolks, vanilla, and coffee and mix by hand. Add butter mixture and beat about 1 minute on high speed.

Add flour and continue to mix until well blended. Drop teaspoon of batter onto a greased cookie sheet and bake in preheated oven, 350 degrees, about 15 minutes.

9 - 10

DAVY CROCKETT KILT A CAJUN

I remember an old Cajun joke: One old Cajun gentleman asked his friend. "What was that Davy Crockett kilt?"

Friend answered, "He kilt hisse'f a Cajun."

"Mon, dat don't right, he killed hisse'f a bear."

"Well," the friend retorted, "if Hebert (pronounced a-bear) don't be a Cajun, what he are?"

OPELOUSAS, LOUISIANA

Opelousas is the third oldest city in Louisiana, established 1720, rich in history and home for many famous people. Calling Opelousas home are Clifton Chenier the King of Zydeco music, Paul Prudhomme famous for his down-home Cajun cooking and his K-Paul Restaurant in

New Orleans and Jim Bowie, inventor of the famed Bowie knife. A cholera epidemic killed Bowie's wife and children. He went to Texas to join in the fight there and died at the Alamo. Visit this little city rich in history, great food and happy people.

720 DROPS OF MAGIC—TABASCO PEPPER SAUCE

BREAKFAST SHIRRED EGGS

Folks, now a few wonderful recipes using the universally famous Tabasco sauce:

Break 2 eggs into a buttered custard cup. In another cup mix 2 tablespoons milk, $^1/_4$ teaspoon salt and $^1/_4$ teaspoon Tabasco pepper sauce. Pour over eggs and bake in 325-degree oven about 15 minutes or until mixture sets.

PIQUANT PECANS

Now a great Tabasco appetizer.

In small pot or skillet, melt 3 tablespoons butter; add 3 cloves minced garlic and $1^1/_2$ teaspoons of Tabasco. Cook for about 60 to 70 seconds. Toss 3 cups shelled pecans with the butter mixture. Spread in a single layer on baking sheet and bake in 250-degree oven for 1 hour, stirring occasionally. Pecans will crisp when cool. Nothing ever tasted so good, I guarantee! Serves 6.

CRAB SOUP A LA TABASCO

1 lb. fresh crabmeat or 2 cans crabmeat
$^1/_3$ cup sherry wine
1 can tomato soup
1 can green pea soup
$^1/_2$ tsp. Tabasco pepper sauce
2 cups half & half or whole milk

In a mixing bowl, combine crabmeat and sherry. Using 3 quart sauce pan stir together soups and Tabasco sauce. Gradually stir in half & half and simmer over low heat. When ready to serve, add crabmeat and bring back to simmer and serve. Serves 6.

HERBED LIME CHICKEN A LA TABASCO

Here's a dish that would have your family and friends coming back and back and back for more and more and more.

In a gallon size plastic bag, combine the following:

2 to 3 lb. cut-up chicken
$^1/_2$ cup vegetable oil
$^1/_3$ cup lime juice
$^1/_4$ cup chopped onion
2 crushed cloves garlic
1 tsp. Tabasco pepper sauce
$^3/_4$ tsp. crumbled dried rosemary
$^1/_2$ tsp. dried marjoram
$^1/_2$ tsp. salt

Slowly turn bag upside down a couple of times to evenly coat the bird. Refrigerate over night or at least 8 hours. Drain chicken and reserve marinade. Grill the chicken about 20 minutes per side or until done. Brush chicken with marinade several times while cooking. Folks, you will simply love this dish.

CHICKEN AND SHRIMP PILOU

We pay homage to the king of hot sauces, the redoubtable product in the little bottle with the diamond label: *Tabasco* pepper sauce.

I learned to make this wonderful dish from an old Creole lady, who moved from Savannah to South Louisiana. It's one of my favorites.

1 (2 lb.) chicken, quartered
1 rib celery, chopped
3 black pepper corns
4 slices thick bacon
1 large onion chopped
1 garlic clove, minced
$1^1/_2$ cups chicken stock or broth
2 tomatoes, peeled and chopped
1 cup long grain rice
1 Tbsp. lemon juice

1 tsp. Worcestershire sauce
$^3/_4$ tsp. Tabasco pepper sauce
$^1/_2$ tsp. ground nutmeg
1 lb. medium shrimp (fresh or frozen) shelled and deveined
1 Tbsp. minced fresh parsley

Put chicken in large saucepan and add 2 cups water and $^1/_2$ teaspoon salt. Add celery and peppercorns and bring to boil. Reduce heat, cover, and simmer for 30 minutes. Transfer chicken to a platter. When cool, skin chicken and pull the meat from the bones and set aside. Preheat oven to 350 degrees. In a large skillet, fry the bacon until crisp. Drain and crumble bacon and reserve 2 tablespoons of the grease.

Heat the 2 tablespoons bacon grease in a heavy 4-quart or larger casserole or Dutch oven. Add onions and garlic and sauté for about 2 minutes. Add rice and stir to coat the rice. Add stock, tomatoes, lemon juice, nutmeg, and Tabasco and stir well until mixture comes to a boil. Cover tightly and put into hot oven and bake for 20 minutes. Remove from oven and stir in the shrimp and crumbled bacon and chicken meat. Return to oven and bake, covered, for 15 minutes. Remove and let stand for 10 to 15 minutes.

Fluff with fork; salt and pepper to taste and sprinkle the parsley over mixture. Food to die for friends Oh boy!

ENOLA'S LOUISIANA CAKE

My friend Chef Paul's sister, Enola Prudhomme, can also lay claim to one of the world's most prestigious titles, "Chef."

Enola Prudhomme's Cajun Cafe in Carencro, just south of Opelousas, is as good as it gets. The following recipe is very close to her Granny Cake recipe in her excellent cookbook, *Low-Calorie Cajun Cooking*. Her brother, Paul, says she "cooks unleaded food."

$^2/_3$ c. cottage cheese
1 c. sugar
1 egg plus 2 egg whites
$^1/_3$ tsp. butter flavoring
2 c. cake flour
1 tsp. baking soda
1 c. crushed canned pineapple, drained

Preheat oven to 350 degrees. Put cottage cheese in blender and process until smooth, set aside. Combine sugar, egg, whites, butter flavor, and cottage cheese. Beat for 1 minute. Combine flour and soda; mix well. Gradually add to cottage mixture and stir in pineapple. Beat well. Pour batter into 8 inch fluted tube pan sprayed with Pam. Bake 30 to 35 minutes or until cakes is done.

Note: You may add $^2/_3$ cup chopped pecans or walnuts to cake batter, if desired.

A nice touch is to press pecan halves or walnut halves in a pattern into iced cake. Let cake cool before icing. See icing recipe below.

ICING ROYAL

This icing recipe is good for cakes, cupcakes, or cookies and licking the bowl.

1 cup cottage cheese
1 cup powdered sugar (white)
4 Tbsp. softened cream cheese
3 Tbsp. soft butter or margarine
1 tsp. vanilla extract

Combine all of the above in mixing bowl and beat on low speed for 3 minutes. Keep pushing the sides back down into the mixing bowl. Makes $1^1/_2$ cups enough for 1 cake or 12 muffins.

Note: Add $^1/_2$ cup chopped nuts, pecans or walnuts

ABOUT BLACKENING

A number of years ago Chef Paul Prudhomme created the blackening process of cooking. The world owes him a vote of thanks. Food has a very fresh and sweet taste when blackened properly and many times it is not done correctly.
A. Blackening should be done outside or in a well-ventilated kitchen. It makes a lot of smoke.
B. Use only a heavy cast iron skillet. You may use any heavy skillet but cast iron works best. I usually rub the skillet with a little olive oil.
C. Skillet should be heated to very hot, about 500 degrees. Allow pan to reheat between batches.

D. It is best if the fish or meat is allowed to get to room temperature before cooking.

E. The fish or meat should go directly from the skillet to the plate to retain all of the blackening and flavor.

BLACKENING

Thank you, Paul Prudhomme, for this style of cooking.

1 Tbsp. paprika
2 tsp. salt 3 sticks melted butter
1 tsp. onion powder (unsalted is best)
1 tsp. garlic powder
1 tsp. cayenne pepper
$^{1}/_{2}$ tsp. ground white pepper
1 tsp. black pepper
$^{1}/_{2}$ tsp. thyme
$^{1}/_{2}$ tsp. oregano
3 sticks melted butter
6 (8 oz.) fillets firm-fleshed fish like tuna, salmon, shark, fresh water catfish, snapper, and of course redfish

Heat butter until liquid in separate pot. Mix seasonings together in small bowl.

Cook one piece at a time. First, dip fillet in the melted butter and sprinkle seasoning mix evenly on both sides. Place fish in hot skillet and cook about 2 minutes. Turn over and cook other side for 2 minutes. Remove to plate and spread 1 teaspoon of butter over side of fish that is up. Serve to wide-eyed dinner guests and accept the kudos. Serves 6.

BLACKENED CHICKEN GUMBO A LA MULATE

Folks, this is one dish that can make you famous in your neighborhood. This recipe comes from the world-famous Cajun restaurant in Beaux Bridge and New Orleans.

Make one of the rouxs we talked about earlier. Blacken 2 to 3 pounds chicken breasts following blackening instructions.

2 c. chopped onions
2 c. chopped bell peppers
1$^{1}/_{2}$ c. chopped celery
$^{1}/_{4}$ c. minced garlic
6 qt. chicken stock
4 c. cut okra
$^{1}/_{2}$ tsp. salt and cayenne pepper

Add onions, bell pepper, celery, and garlic to roux that has been brought to simmer. Simmer about 15 minutes, stirring often. Add stock and simmer for 20 minutes. Add blackened chicken, cut into strips, and okra, salt, and pepper. Simmer for 30 minutes. Remove from heat and let stand for 15 minutes. Serve over white rice. Potato salad or coleslaw and warm French bread make this a meal to remember.

A-BEAR'S CHICKEN AND SAUSAGE GUMBO

When you get to Houma, you'll find A-Bear's Cafe at 809 Bayou Black Road. Stand by to eat. The actual name of the eatery is Hebert's. All of the outlanders always pronounced it wrong. They called it He-bert—wrong. The correct Cajun pronunciation is A-Bear. So, it was just easier for Jane and Curly to use the phonetic, hence A-Bear's.

This is a Cajun traditional gumbo at its best.

2 cups either roux we talked about earlier (see recipe index)
1 large onion, chopped
4 lb. frying chicken cut up
6 cups water
1 pound smoked sausage
$^{1}/_{3}$ cup chopped parsley
$^{1}/_{3}$ cup chopped shallots
1 tsp. file powder
$^{1}/_{2}$ tsp. salt and black pepper

Simmer roux over medium heat. Add chopped onions and simmer 5 minutes. Add the chicken, salt, and pepper and cover with 1 cup water, stirring often and simmer for 30 minutes. Do not boil hard. Add remainder of the water; cover and simmer 30 more minutes. Add sausage, cut into bite-size pieces, and cook additional 15 minutes. It's OK if you have to add a little extra water. Add parsley and shallots and cook with lid off for 5 minutes. Turn off heat and sprinkle file over gumbo, stir, and serve over a bed of white rice. Oh boy! Serves 6.

TUJAGUE'S FAMOUS BOILED BRISKET OF BEEF WITH HORSERADISH SAUCE

Tujague's (pronounced Two-Jacks) has always been one of my favorite purveyors of culinary delights in New Orleans. That says a lot as from the beginning, New Orleans has been an eating town and has some of the best restaurants in the world. Tujague's is one of the oldest restaurants in the city. They began serving the dockworkers in 1856 simple Creole food and haven't slowed down since. Say hello to Steve Latter when you partake of lunch or dinner there.

4 lb. beef brisket
2 medium onions, sliced
2 ribs chopped celery
4 mashed toes (cloves) garlic
3 sprigs parsley
3 bay leaves
$^1/_2$ tsp. thyme
5 Tbsp. salt

Put the beef brisket in a soup pot (heavy-duty pot, not aluminum) having trimmed excess fat. Add the onions, celery, garlic, parsley, bay leaves, thyme, and peppercorns. Cover with water and bring to a boil; turn down heat and simmer slowly for about 3 hours, or until brisket is very tender. Add salt when brisket is about done. Remove brisket from pot; drain and slice. Serve brisket with horseradish sauce.

Horseradish Sauce—blend together:

1 c. horseradish, prepared
$^1/_2$ c. Creole or deli mustard
1 cup ketchup
12 whole black peppercorns

Serves six as an entree or ten as an appetizer.

TUJAGUE'S FAMOUS BREAD PUDDING

2 loaves stale, French bread
$^3/_4$ lb. butter
1 qt. sugar
$^3/_4$ cup vanilla
$^1/_2$ tsp. nutmeg
15 raw eggs
$^1/_4$ cup good brandy
1 quart whole milk
$^1/_2$ cup raisins
1 pint orange juice

Cut French bread into 1 inch thick slices. Randomly fill a large pan or baking dish with bread at least 3 inches deep. Melt the butter and mix all remaining ingredients in large bowl. Pour this mixture on top of the bread and let soak for 5 minutes. Bake in a 350-degree oven for 45 to 50 minutes or till the pudding rises. Top with Tujague's tart cranberry sauce or your favorite sauce. *Wow!* Serve eight to ten.

TUJAGUE'S TART CRANBERRY SAUCE

1 can whole cranberry sauce or 1 lb. fresh cranberries, cooked until
    tender
$^1/_2$ can water
2 Tbsp. vanilla
$^1/_2$ cup good brandy
1 cup sugar
5 Tbsp. cornstarch
$^1/_4$ stick butter

Put into heavy pot and bring all ingredients, except water, cornstarch, and butter, to simmer. Mix in water and cornstarch alternately until a thick creamy consistency is achieved. Add the butter to the hot sauce immediately and serve. (Folks, this sauce is great on many things. Experiment.) Serves eight.

RICE PUDDING

As you already know, Louisiana grows the finest long grain rice in the world. We use rice in many ways, but this is one of my favorites.

$^1/_2$ c. raisins
2 c. cooked white rice
$1^1/_2$ c. milk
1 Tbsp. soft butter
$^1/_3$ to $^1/_4$ c. sugar (to taste)
3 eggs, beaten
1 tsp. vanilla extract
$^1/_2$ tsp. salt
$^1/_3$ tsp. nutmeg
1 tsp. cinnamon

Preheat oven to 325 degrees. Combine rice, milk, butter, sugar, eggs, vanilla, and salt. Blend well. Add nutmeg and raisins. Pour mixture into a greased baking dish and sprinkle top with cinnamon. Bake 50 minutes. Serves 6-8.

Note: A nice variation is to soak the raisins for 30 minutes in about $^1/_4$ cup dark rum before adding to pudding.

REMOULADE SAUCE

From Poor Boy's Riverside Inn located in Lafayette, famous in Louisiana.

1 qt. mayonnaise
$^1/_3$ c. prepared horseradish
$^1/_3$ c. Creole or brown mustard
1 clove garlic, minced
$^1/_2$ cup chopped celery
$^1/_2$ cup chopped onion
1 tsp. paprika

Blend all ingredients together at slow speed for 3 minutes in blender or use hand mixer on medium speed. Serves 8.

REMOULADE SAUCE A LA PRUDHOMME

Paul Prudhomme makes a different Remoulade sauce. It's more complex but is my personal favorite. It's the one I use because of all the different flavors Paul adds.

2 egg yolks
$^1/_3$ c. vegetable oil
$^1/_3$ c. chopped parsley (fresh if available)
$^2/_3$ c. finely chopped celery
$^2/_3$ c. finely chopped green onions
$^1/_3$ c. prepared horseradish
2 crumbled bay leaves
3 Tbsp. brown mustard
1 tsp. fresh lemon juice
3 Tbsp. catsup
2 Tbsp. Worcestershire sauce (Leas & Perrins preferably)
1 Tbsp. white distilled vinegar
1 tsp. Tabasco sauce
1 tsp. garlic powder or 3 fresh cloves, minced
2 tsp. paprika
1 tsp. salt

Using a blender, food processor, or hand mixer, beat the egg yolks for a minute or two. Add the oil slowly in a stream to the mixture. Add each of the remaining ingredients, one at a time, and blend for 3 or 4 minutes. Put sauce into bowl and put into refrigerator. Sauce is better if it chills for 12 or more hours before using. Makes 2 cups.

JOHNNY CAKE

This is the first thing I learned to cook while I was a boy. These cakes may be eaten hot or cold. Legend has it that Johnnycake was prepared by the women of Jean Lafitte's pirates for them to take on a raid, as they didn't like to start a fire on board the ships.

2 c. all-purpose flour
2 Tbsp. baking powder
$^1/_4$ tsp. salt
1 tsp. sugar
1 Tbsp. soft butter
$^1/_3$ cup water
$^1/_2$ cup cooking oil

Mix together flour, baking powder, salt, and sugar. Add water a little at a time. Knead dough with hands. If dough clings to, dust hands with flour. Knead until smooth. Dust cutting board with flour and roll dough into long roll about 2 inches in diameter. Cut into 1 inch pieces and roll each piece into ball about golf ball size. Flatten balls gently with palm of hand.

Cooking with Crazy Charley IV

Heat about half of the oil to medium heat and fry each cake until golden brown on both sides. Drain on paper towel or brown paper bag. It's good, you hear!

Note: You may substitute $^1/_2$ cup cornmeal for $^1/_2$ of the flour.

CHEESE NUTS

As you know, we love pecans and use them in many different ways. This delicious appetizer will delight your guests.

> 2 sticks butter (let stand at room temperature until soft; margarine may be substituted)
> 2 c. extra sharp grated Cheddar cheese
> 1 cup sifted all-purpose flour
> 1 Tbsp. baking powder
> 1 tsp. salt
> $^1/_2$ tsp. cayenne pepper
> 1 cup pecan halves

Preheat oven to 330 degrees. In a large mixing bowl, blend the soft butter and cheese well. Add the rest of the ingredients. On a greased baking sheet, form dough using a teaspoon and place on sheet. Press one half of pecan into each ball, flattening the dough somewhat. Bake about 12 minutes. Yields 50 to 60 pieces.

CLASSIC RED BEANS AND RICE

Red beans and rice is a tasty, hearty meal that is a south Louisiana Monday tradition. Monday has always been washday and red beans and rice was a dish that was put on to cook when you began the washing and was done as you finished the laundry. There are many ways to cook this great dish. The late, great Louis Armstrong loved this dish so much he signed his letters "Red beans and ricely yours."

> 1 lb. dried red or kidney beans
> 4 Tbsp. butter or olive oil
> 1 c. chopped green onions including tops
> $^1/_2$ c. chopped regular onions
> 1 c. chopped celery
> 1 tsp. garlic powder or 3 cloves, minced fresh
> 2 or 3 ham hocks

1 tsp. salt
2 bay leaves
1 tsp. black pepper
1 tsp. white pepper
Cayenne pepper to taste
1 Tbsp. chopped parsley
$^1/_2$ tsp. cumin

Put beans into large bowl and soak overnight, or, do as I do. Put beans and enough cold water to cover the beans; bring to brisk boil for 3 minutes. Turn off and let beans soak for 1 hour. Drain beans and return them to cooking pot, cover with fresh water an inch above beans, and bring to slow boil. This will also take out most of the gas-causing element, that's right beans won't be the "musical fruit" anymore. As the beans begin to boil, in a skillet add the oil or butter and simmer the onions, celery, garlic, and parsley until soft, not brown. Add mixture to beans. Add ham hocks and the rest of the seasonings. Bring to boil, reduce heat partially cover pot, and simmer for 3 hours. The laundry should be done by then and you are ready to eat. You may have to add a little water from time to time. Eat over boiled long grain white rice. Serves 4-6.

Note: When cooked, you may want to remove meat from hocks and give bones to the dog. Also, the many assorted peppers enhance flavor as different types of peppers are tasted in different parts of your mouth and the blend of the peppers excites taste buds.

BLACK-EYED PEAS

It is surprising how many people don't know how to cook good black-eyed peas. When cooked right and served with cornbread, you have a dish good enough to serve anyone.

We always have black-eyed peas on New Year's Day to bring luck throughout the year.

Place 1 pound dried black-eyed peas in a large pan or bowl and cover with about 4 inches of water. Soak overnight.

2 tsp. salt 3 cups chopped onions
1 tsp. garlic powder

2 tsp. black pepper
1 tsp. cumin
2 Tbsp. chopped parsley
1 bay leaf, broken into quarters
3 cups chopped onions
1 cup chopped bell pepper
$^1/_2$ cup chopped celery
$^1/_2$ tsp. cayenne pepper
6 cups water
1 tbsp. olive oil

Drain the peas and set aside.

Using a heavy 6 quart pan sauté onions, bell pepper, and celery until soft. Stir in the stock and all remaining seasonings and the water. Add the peas and stir and simmer, uncovered, for two hours. Add extra water, if needed. C'est bon, you hear!

DEVILED EGGS

6 hard-boiled eggs, crumbled
2 heaping Tbsp. mayonnaise (you may use reduced calorie or reduced fat mayonnaise)
1 tsp. prepared mustard
3 slices crisp bacon, crumbled
$^1/_3$ cup finely chopped onion
8 drops of good Louisiana hot sauce like Tabasco

Slice eggs in halves lengthwise and take out yolks. In a bowl, mash yolks and seasonings. Mash into thick paste.

Stuff the egg whites with mixture and garnish with sliced black olives, parsley sprigs, or sprinkle with paprika. Makes 12 halves.

SKINNY SMASHED POTATOES

I know everyone is eating somewhat lighter today and that's OK by me if the food still tastes good. Here is a recipe for smashed potatoes that is fat-free and only a little over 100 calories per serving. I usually have the skins on the potatoes for the extra nutrition it gives you; that's up to you.

5 medium size good potatoes, washed and cut into 1 inch cubes
1 can fat-free chicken broth or you can skim off the fat
1 Tbsp. garlic powder or 4 cloves minced garlic
3 heaping Tbsp. chopped parsley
1 tsp. Tabasco
1 tsp. salt
1 Tbsp. coarse mustard like deli mustard
1 level tsp. prepared horseradish
$^1/_2$ cup fat-free sour cream

Put cut up potatoes into heavy 4 -quart saucepan. Add stock and garlic, parsley, pepper sauce, and salt. Bring to a slow boil, reduce heat, cover, and simmer for 20 minutes. Stir the mixture several times. If you need more liquid, add a little water. After 20 minutes, begin to mash the potatoes as you stir until liquid is absorbed. Remove from heat; add mustard, horseradish, and sour cream. Serves 6.

CANDIED LOUISIANA YAMS

5 large sweet potatoes or yams
$1^1/_2$ cups well-packed brown sugar
6 Tbsp. butter or margarine
8 Tbsp. orange juice
1 Tbsp. lemon juice
$^1/_3$ cup raisins
$^1/_2$ tsp. salt
1 tsp. nutmeg

Peel potatoes and steam until done. Slice potatoes and place in large Pyrex or large baking dish. In a saucepan, combine remainder of ingredients, except nutmeg, and bring to a slow boil, stirring several times. Pour mixture over potatoes and bake 1 hour in 325-degree oven. Baste 2 or 3 times with syrup. Take dish out of oven and sprinkle with nutmeg. Serves 6-8.

FRIED WHOLE TURKEY

Folks, this is a great way to enjoy the bird that Ben Franklin wanted to make as our national bird.

Maybe you saw Justin Wilson fry a whole turkey on television. Anyway, you're gonna love it!

1 (12 to 15 lb.) turkey
1 tsp. salt
1 tsp. black pepper
1 tsp. red pepper
1 tsp. sage
1 cup strained chicken, turkey or vegetable broth
2 Tbsp. Garlic juice
2 gallons cooking oil (peanut oil preferred)

In a mixing bowl, combine stock, seasonings, and garlic juice. Stir until well mixed. Using a basting needle, inject mixture into flesh of turkey. Most of mixture should be put into the breast.

Use a pot large enough to hold oil and turkey together. Turkey frying pots are available in many cooking or hardware stores. Using a coat hanger wire or similar hard wire, wire the drumsticks together. Form a wire handle attached to drumstick wire to raise and lower turkey into oil.

Heat the oil to 375 degrees in deep fryer. Carefully lower thè bird into the oil. Cover entire bird with hot oil. Fry about 30 minutes. Test for doneness by piercing the thigh. If red, cook 10 minutes longer. It is done if the juice is clear. Carefully lift turkey and place on brown grocery bags or paper towels to drain. Let stand 20 minutes; transfer to turkey platter and enjoy. Serves 8-10.

BEEF STEW A LA JULIUS

There is nothing quite like a hearty beef stew to set the mouth watering and to satisfy the discerning palate. This old time beef stew does it all. It is eaten with rice in my part of the country, and with hot, fresh corn bread. My brother-in-law, Julius Champagne, showed me how to prepare this tasty dish. It will serve 8 hungry folk with a little left over.

4 Tbsp. all-purpose flour
1 tsp. salt
$^1/_2$ c. chopped celery
$^1/_2$ tsp. garlic powder
$^1/_2$ tsp. black pepper
$^1/_2$ tsp. ginger
3 lb. chuck, cut into stewing size pieces
3 Tbsp. vegetable oil (we used bacon fat)
$^1/_2$ tsp. Louisiana hot sauce like Tabasco
1 lb. canned tomatoes

1 (8 oz.) can tomato sauce
3 medium sliced onions
$^1/_3$ c. red wine vinegar
$^1/_2$ c. molasses
6 carrots, cut into 1 inch
$^1/_2$ c. raisins

Using a heavy 4-quart Dutch oven, combine first 6 ingredients and sprinkle onto the beef cubes you have put into Dutch oven. Add the oil or bacon fat and brown well on medium heat, stirring several times, about 20 minutes. Add $^1/_2$ cup water and next 5 ingredients and bring to boil. Cover and turn heat to medium or medium-low and simmer about 2 hours. Remove cover, stir, and add carrots and raisins and a little more water, if needed. Cook until carrots are tender, about 30 minutes. Man, oh man.

I'm going to put a pot on now. If you prefer potatoes, you may add 3 medium potatoes, cleaned and cut into 1 inch squares when you add the carrots.

YAM-SWEET POTATO PIE

Well, shut my mouth!

3 medium yams or sweet potatoes
$^2/_3$ c. brown sugar
$^1/_2$ tsp. salt
$^1/_2$ tsp. allspice
$^1/_2$ tsp. cinnamon
$^1/_4$ tsp. nutmeg
2 eggs, beaten light
1 cup half & half
1/2 tsp. vanilla extract

Bake potatoes; peel and mash. In large mixing bowl, combine all ingredients together. Mix well for about 5 minutes on medium-low. Pour into 9 inch pie shell and bake at 350 degrees for about 40 minutes. Test for doneness as in recipe for pecan pie. Let pie cool about 20 minutes on rack.

Folks, this pie is good both warm and cold. Many a morning when I got up before dawn to go hunting and fishing, my breakfast was hot coffee and a slice of cold yam or sweet potato pie.

SHRIMP SOUP

As we have indicated, we use a lot of seafood in our cooking and a lot of the seafood we use is shrimp. Here is a delicious shrimp soup that is good on hot summer days as well as cold, rainy days.

Sometimes I will add crawfish tails or substitute cod or other whitefish.

1 cup onions, chopped
$^1/_2$ c. bell pepper, chopped
3 large fresh tomatoes chopped up, or a 16 oz. can tomatoes
2 c. fresh corn, chopped off the cob, or a 16 oz. can whole corn
5 pt. cold water
$^1/_2$ tsp. salt
$^1/_2$ tsp. black pepper
1 tsp. Tabasco sauce
$1^1/_2$ lb. shrimp peeled and deveined or crawfish tails or a mix
   of the two
4 slices bacon, fried very crisp crumpled into small bits

The first thing to do is make one of the roux' listed earlier. Use a 4- quart heavy pot to make the roux in. After roux is done, add the onions and bell pepper. Cook slowly for 10 minutes. Add the bacon pieces, tomatoes, and corn. Cover pot and simmer for 15 minutes. Add water and seasonings and bring back to simmer 40 minutes. Add the seafood and cook, uncovered, on low heat for 10 minutes. Let stand for 15 minutes before serving. This soup is also good served cold. Serves 6 people. You may want to garnish with parsley or tops or green onions.

CAJUN BOILED CRAWFISH

Below is the recipe that Stuart Sayes has perfected for boiled crawfish. He was one of the original owners (with Robert) of Louisiana Cajun Crawfish, Inc. Follow it closely, and I promise you'll enjoy this Cajun delicacy. Serves 10-20 people.

Equipment: One very large pot, approximately 18 to 20 gallons, with cover, one propane burner big enough to bring this pot to a boil. A large utensil used to stir the pot (a small paddle, broom handle, or thick, cleaned branch cut to about 3 feet).

Ingredients (in order of use):

$^1/_2$ lb. salt (for cleaning crawfish)

2 oz. ground cayenne pepper

1 pkg. crawfish boil seasoning

5 to 10 lb. small red/Irish potatoes (close to golf ball size or cut into quarters)

5 large yellow onions cut into quarters

4 large lemons cut into halves

24 oz. fresh whole mushrooms (small to medium size)

1 oz.. whole bay leaves

1 clove garlic, diced

1 (40 lb.) sack live Louisiana crawfish

12 half pieces corn (preferably fresh)

Preparation: Thoroughly wash the crawfish in a large "foot tub" by rinsing and draining twice, until rinse water is reasonably clean. Cover crawfish in tub again with water, and add $^1/_2$ pound of salt (the salt is added to purge and clean the crawfish prior to eating). Stir for no longer than 3 minutes and drain water. Immediately fill the tub again with cool water, leaving out the salt, and stir for 3 minutes, then drain (if the crawfish are allowed to soak in the water too long, they will die). Inspect and discard dead crawfish, bait and other debris that may be present. For a 40 pound sack of crawfish, fill an 18 to 20 gallon pot with about 10 gallons of water (or enough water to cover crawfish and vegetables when they are put in). Bring to a boil.

Cooking: Add cayenne pepper and crawfish boil seasoning. Bring mixture to a boil. In the basket (that fits into the pot), place bay leaves, potatoes, lemons, onions, mushrooms, and garlic. Place the basket in the boiling water, and boil these vegetables and seasonings for 10 to 15 minutes, stirring occasionally.

Carefully add live crawfish into the basket, which is already in the pot of boiling water. Stir, cover, and bring back to a boil. Remove cover and let the whole thing boil for 4 minutes. Remove entire pot (with basket in it) from heat (or turn off heat); add corn. Stir and keep uncovered for 5 to 20 minutes. The longer the crawfish are left to stand like this (in excess of 5 minutes), the more seasoned and spicy they will be. You also want to cook them long enough to release them from their shell to make eating them easier.

Start sampling (tasting) the crawfish after 5 minutes (of standing) to achieve the desired taste and consistency. Personally, we recommend that you let the crawfish stand covered until they begin to sink, which means they are thoroughly marinated with the water and seasonings, which is somewhere around 15 to 20 minutes. They should be quite spicy by that time, so be careful.

Modifications—Dips and Sauces: Divide ingredients and make 2 batches to perfect second batch and keep crawfish nice and hot.

Use less spices (or take some crawfish out earlier).

Use more corn and potatoes for the less imaginative members of your group: Cocktail sauce basically ketchup and horseradish, lemon, butter, garlic, or any combination of the above three.

CORNED BEEF SALAD MOLD
from James Raborn

1 (6 oz.) pkg. lemon flavored gelatin
1$^3/_4$ c. boiling water
1 (12 oz.) can corned beef
1 c. finely chopped celery
$^1/_4$ c. finely chopped onion
2 Tbsp. finely chopped green bell pepper
3 hard-boiled eggs, chopped
1 c. mayonnaise or salad dressing

Dissolve gelatin in boiling water—cool. Combine corned beef, chopped vegetables, eggs, and mayonnaise. Stir into gelatin mixture. Spoon into salad mold or Bundt cake pan or an 11$^3/_4$ x 7$^1/_2$ x 1$^3/_4$ inch. Chill. Garnish with tomato wedges, carrot sticks, egg slices, pickles, olives, and parsley.

BEAN-COUNTER SALAD
from Paul L. Kidd

Shred about $^1/_2$ a small jar (or less) of baby sweet gherkin pickles. Mix perhaps a cup of the sweet pickle juice with a half cup of mayonnaise or salad dressing. Make the mixture thicker or thinner by varying the amounts of the last two ingredients. Drain one 12 ounce can of each of garbanzo beans (AKA chickpeas), French cut green beans, and red beans. Mix well, chill, and serve.

BRUSSELS SPROUTS INSIDE AND OUT
from Glen Keller

2 lb. ground beef
$1^1/_2$ c. instant or cooked rice
1 medium onion, chopped
2 eggs, lightly beaten
1 tsp. Cajun powder
1 (10 oz.) pkg. fresh or frozen Brussels sprouts
2 cans (15 oz.) tomato sauce
1 tsp. thyme
1 c. water

In a large bowl, combine first 6 ingredients and mix well. Shape a scant $^1/_4$ cup around each frozen Brussels sprout to form a meatball. Place in a 13x9x1 inch baking dish, do not grease. Combine tomato sauce, water, and thyme. Pour over meatballs. Cover and bake at 350 degrees for 1 hour and 15 minutes or until meat balls are cooked through.

SHRIMP ETOUFFEE
from Margaret Maring

1 c. finely chopped onion
1 c. finely chopped celery
$^1/_2$ c. finely chopped green onions with tops
2 cloves garlic, crushed
$^1/_2$ c. butter
2 Tbsp. flour
2 c. chicken stock
$^1/_2$ c. Ro-Tel hot tomatoes

1 Tbsp. Worcestershire sauce
Salt to taste
1 tsp. ground black pepper
2 lb. peeled shrimp, crawfish or chicken
3 c. cooked white long grain rice

In a heavy Dutch oven, sauté the onion, celery, green onions, and garlic in the butter over medium heat. Cook until the vegetables are soft but not brown. Stir in the flour and cook until light brown, stirring constantly. Add chicken stock slowly while stirring with a wooden spoon. Add the tomatoes and simmer for 10 minutes. Add the salt, pepper, and Worcestershire sauce. Add the shrimp to Etouffee mixture and cook over low heat for 15 minutes. Serve over cooked rice. Serves 6. (Etouffee means smothered in Cajun French.)

SPICY LEMON MOP

3 Tbsp. olive oil
2 Tbsp. lemon juice (fresh preferred)
2 Serrano chiles, stems and seeds removed, minced
2 cloves garlic, minced
2 tsp. chopped parsley or rosemary
Cajun powder to taste

Combine all the ingredients and mix well. Use at room temperature or chill. Use as a mop on asparagus, broccoli, zucchini, or fried or baked fillets of fish.

WILD RICE AND LOUISIANA SAUSAGE

We may live without friends;
We may live without books;
but civilized man cannot live
without cooks!

1 pkg. long grain and wild rice
1 to 1$^1/_2$ lb. Cajun sausage or Louisiana Hot Links
$^1/_2$ cup chopped green onions
$^1/_2$ cup chopped green peppers
$^1/_2$ cup chopped celery
$^1/_2$ cup sliced mushrooms

Cut sausages into one-inch thick rounds. Brown sausage; sauté green onions, peppers, celery and mushrooms. Add to the wild rice mix that has been cooked as directed on package. When sausage has browned and rice still has some liquid to be absorbed, combine both ingredients and simmer until rice is cooked to desired doneness.

THE ART OF SOPPING

When I was a kid and we kids had to eat in the kitchen. Paw Paw would eat with us more often than with the adults in the dining room.

"Paw Paw, why aren't you at the big table?" I would ask.

"Well, son," he replied "your mama don't like me sopping at the table when company is here."

Paw Paw liked to sop, especially as he was 85 and had no teeth. He really liked to take one of Mama's icebox rolls, pour coffee from his cup into his saucer, blow on it to cool it, and then sop it up with the roll. Right, Mama didn't like him to do that, anytime.

I learned the art of sopping from Paw Paw and I'm proud of it.

Sopping can be done using any bread, roll, or cookie dipped into gravy, syrup, coffee, chocolate, or just any kind of juice that is good to eat.

If you want to try sopping, I recommend using cream and syrup.

1 plate with a ridge or soup bowl
4 oz. pure blue ribbon sugar cane syrup (maple syrup will do if that's all you have available)
4 oz. heavy, pure cream

Pour cream and syrup into bowl and sop up with hot roll, toast, biscuit, or even a piece of light bread. Man, that's heaven! You have now learned the art of sopping and your life will never be the same. *Charley*

Charley loves to sop so much he often eats left over cornbread or biscuits for breakfast with maple syrup, and he loves to cover toast with left over spaghetti sauce. I think what he loves the most is to soak up cornbread in pot liquor, the liquid left from cooking greens such as turnip, chard, or mustard. I have even found him eating beans for breakfast, juice, and all poured over anything he could find. He learned that beans are great for breakfast as a submarine sailor. He also learned the best Marine is a submarine. He just loved SOS in the Navy, probably more than any other sailor, because he got to sop biscuits with the meat gravy. I make a mean SOS that he really loves; he often requests it for breakfast when we have overnight guests. (An insider's observation of Charley by Ruth.)

THE ROAD TO YESTERDAY

Friends, I have a copy of an old cookbook published by F. F. Hansell & Bro., Ltd., New Orleans. This out-of-print work carries a copyright date of 1885! It is called *La Cuisine Creole*. I am going to give you some cooking quotes from it. I think you will get a *kick* out of them.

"*La Cuisine Creole* (Creole cookery) partakes of the nature of its birthplace, New Orleans is cosmopolitan in its nature, blending the characteristics of the American, French, Spanish, Italian, West Indian, and Mexican. In this compilation will be found many original recipes and other valuable ones heretofore unpublished, notably those of Gombo file, Bouille-abaisse, Courtbouillon, Jambolaya, Salade a la Russe, Bisque of Crayfish a la Creole, Pousse Cafe, Cafe Brule, Brulot, together with many confections and delicacies for the sick, including a number of mixed drinks. Much domestic contentment depends upon the successful preparation of the meal; and as food rendered indigestible through ignorance in cooking often creates discord and unhappiness, it behooves the young housekeeper to learn the art of cooking.

"Soup being the first course served at all ordinary dinners we make it the basis for preliminary remarks. Nothing more palatable than good, well-made soup and nothing less appetizing than pour soup. Now to attain perfection in any line, care and attention are requisite, careful study a necessity, and application the moving force. Hence, cooking in all its branches should be studied as a science, and not be looked upon as a haphazard mode of getting through life. Cooking is in a great measure a chemical process, and the ingredients of certain dishes should be as carefully weighed and tested as though emanating from the laboratory. Few female cooks think of this, but men with their superior instinctive reasoning power are more governed by law and abide more closely to rule; therefore, are better cooks, and command higher prices for services."

(Remember, this was written in 1885, most certainly by a man. Comment by Charley. Ruth says, "Thanks, Charley.")

175

THE CAJUN KITCHEN

While there are not many differences in a Cajun kitchen and any other American kitchen, there are a few. One thing good South Louisiana cooks will have in their kitchen is a good variety of spices and herbs...and they must be fresh! We usually keep them tightly sealed in small jars like pimiento, baby food, or purchase them already in jars.

The seasonings that we keep in our kitchens and use frequently are:

Tabasco sauce
Crushed red pepper
Black and white pepper
Whole bay leaves
Oregano and tarragon
Sage and celery seed
Powdered cayenne peppers
Chili powder
Garlic
Rosemary
Basil and thyme
Allspice and nutmeg
Cumin and cloves
Gumbo file (ground sassafras leaves)

We always keep what is fondly known as "The Holy Trinity," celery, bell peppers, and onion available at all times. A Cajun couldn't cook anything without them.

Several kinds of pots and saucepans of different sizes are necessary in a well equipped kitchen. I prefer the old iron pots and skillets that have been seasoned properly. (Wiped down with a good vegetable oil after each use and allowed to "season" while stored.) However, copper lined stainless steel utensils are excellent. Also many cast iron utensils coated with porcelain are good. These are frequently used in European kitchens but may be purchased in good cookware and hardware stores here.

While in Lafayette, visit the Acadian Village. It serves as a monument to the proud culture of the Acadian people.

ARE YOU CAJUN? A TEST

Here is how to tell a full-blooded, dipped-in-the-bayou Cajun from someone who just wishes they were one. (Adapted from the writing of Hilda Gallassero; found on Mulate's Cajun Restaurant's menu in Breaux Bridge.)

1. Did your grandmother regularly eat couche-couche for breakfast?

2. Does your father consider a 6 pack of beer and a pound of boudin to be a 7 course meal?

3. Does your grandmother bellyache all week long—until Saturday, when she steps out with the best of them cutting a fine two-step at a Fais Do Do?

4. If the doctor told you coffee causes cancer, would you rather take your chances than do without it? (Not to worry; you'd still get it in your gravy and sauces.)

5. Could you paddle a pirogue 20 miles an hour down a straight stretch of stump free bayou?

6. Is there a Tee-Jean, a Tee-Man, or Tee-Boy among your uncles?

7. Have you always called your uncle by his "Tee" name and forgotten his real one?

8. Are you related to your next door neighbor?

9. Does someone in your family know how to treat sunstroke, the "waste-away sickness" or "Indian Fire"?

10. Can you remember when you hated to tell strangers you'd eaten crawfish for dinner because it was inelegant and everybody knew that only Cajuns ate crawfish?

11. Look closely at the wedding photograph of your grandmother. Was her bridal bouquet made of crepe paper?

12. If someone steps on your toe, would you instinctively yell "Oh, Yee-Yii" instead of ouch?

To score, give yourself 1 point for every "yes" answer. 10 to 12: Full blooded Cajun. 7 to 9: Can't be considered a real Cajun and it is understandable that you may be wrestling with the pains of an identity crisis. 0 to 6: Not even in the ball game.

HAVE YOU CAUGHT THE ESSENCE AND SPIRIT OF CAJUN LAND AND HER PEOPLE?
by Ruth

If you failed the test, I believe everyone deserves a second chance. If you can pass the following test, you have caught the essence of Cajun land and the spirit of the Cajuns.

1. In what state do most Cajuns live in?
2. From which European country did the original Cajuns (Acadians) migrate?
3. What is the difference between a Cajun and a Creole?
4. Name 3 cities or towns in Cajun country.
5. Who was Jean Lafitte?
6. Can you name a famous Cajun chef?
7. Do you know how to eat a crawfish?
8. Have you listened to or danced to the music of a Cajun band?
9. Have you eaten fried catfish and hush puppies, jambalaya, or gumbo?
10. Do you need a cup of coffee to get your heart started in the morning?
11. Have you eaten shrimp cooked in crab boil?
12. Which of the following surnames is Cajun? Smith, Jones, Zabroski, Hebert?

Score your test 1 point for a correct answer; consider yes, correct and no, wrong. 10 to 12: You are an adopted Cajun. 7 to 9: You need more time in Cajun country: eating, touring, and talking to Cajuns. 0 to 6: You are definitely an "outlander." Get to Cajun country as soon as possible to see, hear, taste, smell and feel the essence of Cajun country and catch the spirit of the Cajuns. Answers to the questions 1-7 and 12 are in the book; 8-11 are about Cajun experiences you have had.

Another difference between Cajuns and Creole is that a Cajun can feed three families on one chicken and a Creole feeds one family with three chickens.

THINGS A TRUE SOUTHERNER KNOWS

The difference between a hissie fit and a conniption fit.
Pretty much how many fish make up a mess.
What general direction cattywumpus is.
That "gimme sugar" don't mean pass the sugar.

When somebody's "fixin'" to do something, it won't be long.
The difference between Yankee's and damn Yankee's
How good a cold grape Nehi and cheese crackers are at a country store.
Knows what, "Well I Suwannee!" means.
Ain't nobody's biscuits like Grandma's biscuits!
A good dog is worth its weight in gold.
Real gravy don't come from the store.
The War of Northern Aggression was over state's rights, not slavery.
When "by and by" is.
How to handle their "pot likker."
The difference between "pert' near" and "a right far piece."
The differences between a redneck, a good ol' boy, and trailer trash.
Never to go snipe hunting twice.
At one point learned what happens when you swallow tobacco juice.
You may wear long sleeves, but you should always roll 'em up past the elbows.
You should never loan your tools, pick-up, or gun to nobody.
A belt serves a greater purpose than holding Daddy's pants up.
Rocking chairs and swings are guaranteed stress relievers.
Rocking chairs and swings with an old person in them are history lessons.

GOD BLESS DIXIE!

MOVING TO THE SOUTH?

If you are from the Northern states and planning on visiting or moving to the South, there are a few things you should know that will help you adapt to the difference in lifestyles:

The North has sun-dried toe-mah-toes,
The South has 'mater samiches.

The North has coffee houses,
The South has Waffle Houses.

The North has dating services,
The South has family reunions.

The North has switchblade knives,
The South has Lee Press-on Nails.

The North has double last names,
The South has double first names.

The North has Ted Kennedy,
The South has Billy Graham.

The North has an ambulance,
The South has an amalance.

The North has Indy car races,
The South has stock car races.

The North has Cream of Wheat,
The South has grits.

The North has green salads,
The South has collard greens.

The North has lobsters,
The South has crawfish.

The North has the rust belt,
The South has the Bible Belt.

Don't be surprised to find movie rentals and bait in the same store... Don't buy food at this store.

Remember, "y'all" is singular, "all y'all" is plural, and "all y'all's" is plural possessive.

Get used to hearing "You ain't from round here, are ya?"

You may hear a Southerner say "Ought!" to a dog or child. This is short for "Y'all ought not do that!" and is the equivalent of saying "No!"

Don't be worried at not understanding what people are saying. They can't understand you either.

The first Southern statement to creep into a transplanted Northerner's vocabulary is the adjective "big ol'" truck or "big ol'" boy. Most Northerners begin their Southerner influenced dialect this way. All of them are in denial about it.

The proper pronunciation you learned in school is no longer proper.

Be advised that "He needed killin'" is a valid defense here.

If you hear a Southerner exclaim, "Hey, y'all, watch this," you should stay out of the way. These are likely to be the last words he'll ever say.

When you come up on a person driving 15 mph down the middle of the road, remember that most folks learn to drive on a John Deere, and that is the proper speed and position for that vehicle.

Do not be surprised to find that 10-year-olds own their own shotguns; they are proficient marksmen, and their mammas taught them how to aim.

And remember: If you do settle in the South and bear children, don't think we will accept them as Southerners. After all, if the cat had kittens in the oven, we wouldn't call 'em biscuits.

A RED MARBLE
Author Unknown

During the waning years of the depression in a small southwestern Louisiana community, I used to stop by Mr. Miller's roadside stand for farm-fresh produce as the season made it available. Food and money were still extremely scarce and bartering was used, extensively.

One particular day Mr. Miller was bagging some early potatoes for me. I noticed a small boy, delicate of bone and feature, ragged but clean, hungrily appraising a basket of freshly picked green peas. I paid for my potatoes but was also drawn to the display of fresh green peas. I am a pushover for creamed peas and new potatoes. Pondering the peas, I couldn't help overhearing the conversation between Mr. Miller and the ragged boy next to me.

"Hello Barry, how are you today?"

"H'lo, Mr. Miller. Fine, thank ya. Jus' admirin' them peas...sure look good."

"They are good, Barry. How's your Ma?"

"Fine. Gittin' stronger alla' time."

"Good. Anything I can help you with?"

"No, Sir. Jus' admirin' them peas."

"Would you like to take some home?"

"No, Sir. Got nuthin' to pay for 'em with."

"Well, what have you to trade me for some of those peas?"

"All I got's my prize marble here."

"Is that right? Let me see it."

"Here 'tis. She's a dandy."

"I can see that. Hmmm, only thing is this one is blue and I sort of go for red. Do you have a red one like this at home?"

"Not 'zackley...but, almost."

"Tell you what. Take this sack of peas home with you and next trip this way let me look at that red marble."

"Sure will. Thanks, Mr. Miller."

Mrs. Miller, who had been standing nearby, came over to help me. With a smile she said: "There are two other boys like him in our community, all three are in very poor circumstances. Jim just loves to bargain with them for peas, apples, tomatoes, or whatever. When they come back with their red marbles, and they always do, he decides he doesn't like red after all and he sends them home with a bag of produce for a green marble or an orange one, perhaps."

I left the stand, smiling to myself, impressed with this man. A short time later I moved to Colorado but I never forgot the story of this man, the boys and their bartering. Several years went by each more rapid than the previous one.

Just recently I had occasion to visit some old friends in that Louisiana community and while I was there learned that Mr. Miller had died. They were having his viewing that evening and knowing my friends wanted to go, I agreed to accompany them.

Upon our arrival at the mortuary we fell into line to meet the relatives of the deceased and to offer whatever words of comfort we could. Ahead of us in line were three young men. One was in an army uniform and the other two wore nice haircuts, dark suits, and white shirts...very professional looking.

They approached Mrs. Miller, standing smiling and composed, by her husband's casket. Each of the young men hugged her, kissed her on the cheek, spoke briefly with her and moved on to the casket.

Her misty light blue eyes followed them as, one by one, each young man stopped briefly and placed his own warm hand over the cold pale hand in the casket. Each left the mortuary, awkwardly, wiping his eyes.

Our turn came to meet Mrs. Miller. I told her who I was and mentioned the story she had told me about the marbles. Eyes glittering she took my hand and led me to the casket.

"Those three young men, who just left, were the boys I told you about. They just told me how they appreciated the things Jim "traded" them. Now, at last, when Jim could not change his mind about color or size...they came to pay their debt. "We've never had a great deal of the wealth of this world," she confided, "but, right now, Jim would consider himself the richest man in Louisiana."

With loving gentleness she lifted the lifeless fingers of her deceased husband. Resting underneath were three, magnificently shiny, red marbles.

Moral: We will not be remembered by our words, but by our kind deeds. Life is not measured by the breaths we take, but by the moments that take our breath.

A BRIEF HISTORY OF MARDI GRAS

The "New Orleans version" of Mardi Gras is celebrated in Lafayette, Lake Charles, Houma, and other communities, came to North America from Paris in 1699, when French explorer Iberville and his men explored the Mississippi River. On a spot 60 miles south of what become the location of New Orleans, they set up camp on the river's west bank. Knowing that the day, March 3, was being celebrated as a major holiday in France, they christened the site *Pointe du Mardi Gras*. Mardi Gras celebration is a part of Louisiana's French heritage. Throughout the years, Orleanians have added to the Celebration by establishing Krewes (organizations that host parades and balls). This Carnival quickly became an exciting holiday for both children and adults.

Mardi Gras means "Fat Tuesday" (in French) and is celebrated on that day of the week. The date can fall between February 3 and March 9, depending on the Catholic Church. Mardi Gras is always 47 days before Easter Sunday.

A costumed band of revelers presented the first documented "parade" in 1837. Violent behavior of maskers during the next two decades caused the press to call for an end to Mardi Gras. However, six New Orleanians who were former members of the Cowbellians (a group of New Year's Eve paraders in Mobile) formed the Comus organization in 1857. The men beautified the celebration and proved it could be enjoyed in a festive manner. Comus coined the work "krewe" and established several Mardi traditions by forming a secret carnival society, staging a ball, and presenting a themed parade with floats and costumed maskers.

Krewes today receive their names from the worlds of Greek, Roman, and Egyptian mythology (Orpheus, Apollo, etc.); from the neighborhoods through which they travel or from historical figures or places (Bonaparte). Private carnival krewes hold a series of parties and pageants starting at the beginning of Mardi Gras season, January 6 this year, the Feast of the Epiphany. On this day is the traditional cutting of the King Cake.

The King Cake, or *Gateau du Roi,* dates back to the 12th century France, when the cake was baked on the eve of the Epiphany -the Church feast day that commemorates the three kings' visit to the Christ child, 12 days after his birth. (The word epiphany means, appearance or manifestation of a divine being.) A small token was hidden in the cake as a surprise for the finder. The King Cake was brought to Louisiana by French settlers in the 18th Century.

King Cake colors—purple, green, and gold—are the official colors of Mardi Gras and is a common color theme. In 1872, King Rex, the King of New Orleans' carnival, selected these colors as the official colors of Mardi Gras.

Purple represents justice.
Green stands for faith.
Gold stands for power.

The Mardi Gras season begins about two weeks before Fat Tuesday. During those two weeks, parades can be viewed nightly and on weekends. Almost all businesses are closed for Lundi Gras (Fat Monday) and for Mardi Gras (Fat Tuesday). People come to New Orleans from all over the world to enjoy this extravagant holiday. People come to other cities where Mardi Gras is celebrated, such as Lafayette, Houma, and Mobile, Alabama.

For more information search the following web sites: Mardigrasday.com, Mardi-graszone.com, theholidayspot.com/mardigras, Mardigraswest.com, Acadianhouse.com.

For Mardi Gras decorations: Mardigrasstore.com, Accentannex.com, beadsbythedozen.com.

MARDI GRAS

Celebrate before Lent in the tradition of the Cajun and Creoles in Louisiana. Lent is a religious observance, a time of sacrifice by doing without some pleasures for 40 days before Easter. So, the celebration or Mardi Gras is a big, big party equal to 40 days of parties.

Invite some friends to share the celebration, decorate with balloons, beads and masks, eat Cajun and Creole cuisine, and play some good jazz, zydeco or Cajun music.

CAJUN STORIES

DEAR LORD

So far today, am I doing all right?

I have not gossiped, lost my temper, yelled, been greedy, selfish, nasty, grouchy, or self-indulgent. I have not whined, complained, cursed, or eaten any chocolate. I have charged nothing to my credit card.

But I will be getting out of bed in a minute, and I think that I will really need your help then.

PURPOSE OF THE COOKBOOK

"The intentions of every other piece of prose may be discussed and even mistrusted; but the purpose of a cookery book is one and unmistakable, its object can conceivably be no other than to increase the happiness of mankind."—Joseph Conrad

ACADIANS

The word "Cajun" applies only to those whose Acadian ancestors came to Louisiana after the eviction from Acadia, in 1755. The broader term "Acadian" applies to all the descendants of the original Acadians, regardless of where they now live. Thus, all Cajuns are Acadians, but not all Acadians are Cajuns. Thousands of Acadians live in different parts of the United States and Canada. These people do not speak Cajun. For more information contact: Rev. Msgr. Jules O. Daigle, Swallow Publications, P.O. Box 10, Ville Platte, LA 70586.

THE FLAT TIRE
from Darrell Degenhart

Bubba had a flat tire. He pulled off to the side of the road and proceeded to put one bouquet of flowers in front of his pickup truck and one behind it. Then he just stood back and waited.

A passerby from the city studied the scene as he drove by and was so curious he turned around and went back. He asked Bubba what the problem was. Bubba replied, "Flat tire."

The passerby asked, "But what's with the flowers?" Bubba responded, "When ya break down, they tell ya to put flares in the front and flares in the back. I ain't never understood it neither."

THE PHONE CALL
from Thurston Hahn, Amite, LA

A Cajun couple was asleep when the phone rang at 2 A.M. The wife picked up the phone, listened a moment, and said, "How am I to know? Dat's 200 miles from here!"

The husband asked, "Who dat?"

The wife said, "I don' know. Some woman wants to know if the coast is clear."

IN GOVERNMENT CLASS AT LSU

Margaret Sue was sitting in her U.S. government class at LSU. The professor asked her if she knew what Roe v. Wade was about. Margaret Sue pondered the question, then finally said, "That was the decision George Washington had to make before he crossed the Delaware."

ABRAHAM LINCOLN SAID

"You cannot strengthen the weak by weakening the strong. You cannot help small men by tearing down big men. You cannot help the poor by destroying the rich. You cannot lift the wage earner by pulling down the wage-payer. You cannot keep out the trouble by spending more than your income. You cannot further the brotherhood of man by inciting class hatreds. You cannot build character and courage by taking away a man's initiative and independence. You cannot help men permanently by doing for them what they could and should do for themselves."

THUNDER AND LIGHTNING STORM

Broussard walked to and from elementary school. The weather one morning looked bad, with clouds forming, but he made his daily walk to school. As the day progressed, the winds began to blow, along with thunder and lightning. Following the roar of thunder, lightning would cut through the sky like a flaming sword. Broussard's mother worried that he would be frightened as he walked home from school, and she feared that the electrical storm might harm him.

His mother quickly got into her car and drove along the route to Broussard's school. She saw him walking along, but at each flash of lightning, he would stop, look up, and smile. Another and another followed quickly, and with each flash Broussard would look at the streak of light and smile.

When the mother's car drew up beside him, she lowered the window and called to him, "What are you doing? Why do you keep stopping?" Broussard answered, "I am trying to look nice. God keeps taking my picture."

THE FURNITURE MART

I have fond memories of the late Justin Wilson telling me the following tale around 1960.

It seems that Tejon owned the only furniture store in town. One day as I (Justin) was walking down the street, I saw Tejon bearing himself up the street. He got close to me and yelled, "Justin, me, I'm glad to see you this day, I guarantee."

"Tejon, what's the matter with you? You drunk already and it's only 10 A.M. in the morning?" I asked.

"No, man, I got something to tell you man—*wow!*—it was what you call an adventure."

"Well, told me and calm yoself down."

"Well, Justin, I have the only furniture store in town, you know?"

"Yeah, I know that—everybody knows that. So what?"

"You just stand there and make like you ain't doing nothing and listen, you hear?"

"O.K. Told me your tale," I replied.

"You see, I was looking at this furniture magazine when I saw an ad for the World Furniture Mart. It was at a place called Chicago—me, I determined to take myself there. So, I got in my pirogue and paddled across the bayou and shimmied up the bank and waited by the highway for that doggie bus—you know, that Greyhound—to come along. Well, I got to New Orleans, went to the train station, and got on board the train called the City of New Orleans. Well, Justin, we rode for a long time and finally got to Chicago. Mon oh mon, Justin, that is a biggest place I ever saw.

"So I get in this taxi cab and it took me to my hotel and this man behind the desk said I had to write my name in the register so I did and he passed my key on to me. I went over the alligator, you know, what take you up to your room. Oh boy!—the most beautimus female maiden lady I never see again in my life gets on that same alligator. Well, you know I am a Southern gentleman so it took me 40-30 seconds to say, 'Honey, let's me and you go out and have a cocktail, yeah?' Well, Justin, I found out she from Paris, France, and don't understand my Cajun French, so I reached in my pocket and pulled out my note pad and pencil. I draw two people what sit at a little table with two glasses with straws coming out. I pass that on her face and she takes one look and says, 'We,' and I say, 'Ah low.' We puts our stuff in our rooms and go for them cocktails and maybe five or four just like that. I say, 'Honey, let's me and you get some supper.' She don't understand a thing I said. I reach in my pocket, take out my pad and paper, and draw two people sitting at a table with plates of steaming food. She said, 'We,' I said, 'Ah low and let's go,' and we did.

"Justin, I could tell that maiden lady get very graceful, you know. I say, 'Honey, let's me and you go dance, huh?' She don't understand nothing. I reach in my pocket, pull out my pad and my pencil, and draw two people what dance up close, close, close, you hear? I pass that pad on her face and she smiled and said, 'We we.' I said, 'Ah low, let's go.'

"Oh man, that female maiden lady graceful as I thought. We danced to about 3 or 2 A.M. and I could tell the time was right. I take her arm and lead her out of the club, get a taxi cab, and go back to our hotel. We get the keys and go to the alligator, and go up to her floor. We ge' to her door, she pass her keys on to me, and I open her door for her. I try to pass them key back to her, but she don't understand a damn ting. She reach in my pocket, pull out my pad and my pencil, and drew the most beautiful antique bed I never see again in my life. Justin, I'm still trying to figure out how she knew I was in the furniture business."

THIBODAUX AND BOUDREAUX
from Thurston Hahn

Thibodaux: Did you get dat parrot I sen' you for your birthday?
Boudreaux: Yep, an' it was good! Yeah!
Thibodaux: You ate dat bird?
Boudreaux: Course I ate it.
Thibodaux: That bird spoke five different languages!
Boudreaux: Den he shoulda said somethin'.

WHAT'S DA SCOAH?

Thibodaux: Boudreaux, what's da scoah?
Boudreaux: Seven to ten.

Thibodaux: Who's winnin'?
Boudreaux: Da ten!

BAYOU WATER

When Boudreaux got home yesterday, Clotile ran out to him sayin', "Da cah got water in da carboratah!"

"How you know dat, you?"

"Cause it's pahked in da bayou!"

BOUDREAUX SELLS HIS TRUCK

Boudreaux told Thibodaux he was havin' trouble sellin' his truck, with 200,000 miles on it, for $1,500.

Thibodaux tole him to set the odometer back to 50,000 miles to make it easier to sell.

A few days later Thibodaux asked Boudreaux if he had sold his truck.

"No," replied Boudreaux, "I decided to kept it. It only got 50,000 miles on it."

LOST IN THE WOODS

Boudreaux and Thibodaux went hunting and got lost in the swamp.

When Boudreaux began lamenting their fate, Thibodaux said, "You know, I heard the best thing to do if you get lost is to fire three shots in the air."

So they did that, and waited a while.

When no rescue party showed up, they fired three more shots in the air.

Finally, when there was still no response, Thibodaux said, "Well, I guess we better fire three more shots."

"O.K., if you say so," said Boudreaux. "But somebody better come soon—we're about out of arrows!"

DEAR INTERNAL REVENUE SERVICE

Dere was da time Boudreaux was having trouble sleeping at night.

Boudreaux wrote a letter to the Internal Revenue Service.

He put, "Dear Internal Revenue Service, For da tax year 1993 I underpaid my federal income tax and ain't been able to sleep well since. Enclosed is a check for $200.00. Signed, Yours in Good Government, Boudreaux.

"Mais, P.S. If I don't sleep better tonight, I'm gonna send you da rest."

A GOOD AGGIE JOKE

Boudreaux is sitting in the City Bar in Mauriceville, Louisiana, one Saturday night and has several beers under his belt.

After a while, he looks at the guy sitting next to him, and asks him, "Hey, you wanna hear a good Aggie joke, you?"

The big guy replies, "Let me tell you something. I'm an oilfield roughneck, I weigh 270 pounds, and I don't like Cajuns. My buddy here is a pro football player, weighs 300 pounds, and he doesn't like Cajuns either. His friend on his other side is a professional wrestler, weighs 320 pounds, always has a chip on his shoulder, and he likes Cajuns even less than we do, and we are all Aggies. Do you really want to tell us an Aggie joke?"

Boudreaux, all 150 pounds of Cajun attitude, tells him, "Well, I guess not. I don't want to have to splain it three times."

THE COACHES

The high school coaches in Terrebonne Parish, Louisiana, go to a coaches' retreat. To save money they have to room together. No one wants to room with Coach Boudreaux because he snores so bad. They decide it's not fair to make one of dem stay wit' him the whole time, so they vote to take turns.

Coach Fontenot sleeps with him first, and he come to breakfast next morning hair a mess, eyes all bloodshot. They say, "Man, what happen to you?" He say, "Man, that Boudreaux snore so loud, I watch him all night."

Next night is Coach Guidry's turn. In the morning, same thing—hair all standing up, eyes all bloodshot. They say, "Man, what happen to you? You look awful!"

He say, "Man, dat Boudreaux shake the roof. I watched him all night."

Third night is Coach Breaux's turn. Next morning he come to breakfast bright eyed and bushy tailed. He say, "Good morning, you all." They can't believe!

They say, "Man, what happen?" He say, "Well, we get ready for bed. I go and tuck Boudreaux into bed and kiss him good night. He watch me all night long."

CAJUN 10 COMMANDMENTS

1. Dere jus' be one God in dat Heaven!
2. Don' be having no idols.

3. Don' be cussin' at nobody.
4. Brought yoself to church when dey open da doors.
5. Listen to you ma an' pa.
6. Don' kilt nobody.
7. Ma chere, don' sleep with you brother's wife.
8. Don' go toke nothing from nobody.
9. Always tole da whole troot.
10. Don' go wish fo you neighbor's pirogue or tings.

YOU MIGHT BE CAJUN IF...

1. Watching "Wild Kingdom" inspires you to write a cookbook.
2. You won't eat a lobster because you think it's on crawfish steroids.
3. You take a bite of five-alarm Texas chili and reach for some Tabasco.

HITCHHIKING IN A LOUISIANA RAINSTORM

A stranger from Yankee country was on the side of the road hitchhiking on a very dark night in the middle of a rainstorm that can be experienced only in Louisiana. The night passed slowly and no cars went by. The storm was so strong he could see only a few feet ahead. Suddenly he saw a car slowly looming, ghostlike, out of the gloom. It crept toward him and stopped. Reflexively, the stranger got into the car and closed the door, then realized there was nobody behind the wheel. The car slowly started moving again. The stranger was terrified, too scared to think of jumping and running. The guy saw that the car was slowly approaching a sharp curve. The man started to pray, begging for his life; he was sure the ghost car would go off the road and he would plunge to his death. Just before the curve, a hand appeared through the window and turned the steering wheel, guiding the car safely around the bend.

Paralyzed with terror, the man watched the hand reappear every time they reached a curve. Finally, the man gathered his wits, leaped from the car, and ran into town.

Wet and in shock, he went into a bar. Voice quavering, he ordered two shots of bourbon and told everybody about his horrible, supernatural experience. A silence enveloped everybody when they realized the man was apparently sane and not drunk.

While the man was drinking his bourbon, two local boys walked into the bar. One says to the other, "Look, Boudreaux, dat's dat idiot dat rode in our car when we was pushin' it in de rain."

BOUDREAUX SAYS TO HIS WIFE

You know, dear, when I lost my job, you were right there with me. When we lost the house, you were right there with me. When I had an automobile accident, you were right there with me.

I think you're bad luck.

GLOSSARY

Every region of our diverse country has their own terms for foods, sayings, customs, and ways of life. This is never more apparent than in "Cajun" Country. Even when the people of Acadia speak English, it sounds different. Here are some terms used often in cooking, social communication, and conversation in a Cajun's daily life.

Almondine: A style of cooking using toasted almonds.

Andouille: Sausage made with smoked pork and is popular in Louisiana.

Baste: To moisten roasting meat or other food while baking or grilling by pouring fat drippings or sauce over it.

Bayou: A slow running river of fresh water that runs into another river or into the Gulf of Mexico.

Beignets: Light yeast donuts without holes and covered with powdered sugar a tradition at Cafe Du Monde, New Orleans.

Bisque: A roux based rich soup usually made with crawfish.

Blackened Seasoning: Used for blackened red fish, also used to blacken other foods. A cooking process where fish and meats are cooked in a cast iron skillet that's hot, hot after being dredged in butter and spices.

Blanch: To pour boiling water over a food, then drain and rinse in cold water.

Blend: To mix 2 or more ingredients so that each loses its identity.

Boudin: Pronounced "Boo-dan." A type of sausage made in Southwest Louisiana by combining rice, pork, kidney, spleen, green onions, and parsley, highly seasoned and stuffed into a natural sausage casing. It may be "blanc" white or "rouge" red.

Bourre: A card game where you play for a pot of money.

Broil: To cook by exposing the food directly to the heat source.

Café Brulot: Coffee with brandy and orange peel.

Café Noir: Black Coffee.

Café au Lait: Coffee with milk or cream.

Cajun: Acadians who settled in the swamps and bayou country of Southwest Louisiana after the English deported them from Acadia, Nova Scotia in 1755, also the name of their cuisine and language.

Charwari: A celebration for those who marry late in life.

Chicory: Roasted white chicory root, dried, ground and added to Creole or New Orleans coffee.

Crab & Shrimp Boil: (Also for crawfish.) Several spices put together in a small net bag or ground to a powder to season water for cooking shell fish.

Creole: A person descended from the original French settlers of Louisiana often blended with Spanish, Negro, and Caribbean. Many live in or near New Orleans also, the name of their cuisine and language.

Dredge: To coat with flour

Etouffee (ay-too-fay): A method of cooking almost anything (meats, vegetables or ?) smothered with a liquid, i.e. gravy or a sauce.

File (fee-lay): A powder made from dried sassafras leaves and used as a flavoring and thickening agent.

French Quarter: The original settlement or town where French first settled to establish the city of New Orleans. Many old French homes, hotels, and restaurants have been maintained for locals and tourists to enjoy the *Vieux Carre.*

Garnish: To ornament with something bright and savory. Something added to decorate, such as parsley.

Gumbo: A dish made with okra and file gumbo or both. Recipe came from Bantu tribe of Africa with the slave trade, means "Okra Stew".

Jambalaya (jum-buh-lie-yah): A traditional one pot dish of rice highly seasoned and strongly flavored with combinations of beef, pork, chicken, ham, sausage, or seafood. Word comes from the French "jambon" meaning ham, the African "ya" meaning rice and the Acadian language where everything is "a la." (From Acadian Dictionary, 1981, Rita and Gabrielle Claudet, Houma, LA.)

Jax: Jackson Brewery is where Jax, the beer, was brewed in New Orleans, Louisiana for many years. No longer brewed, the building is now the home of over 50 specialty shop, a Creole and Cajun cooking experience, gifts, and souvenirs.

Julienne: To cut into match like strips.

Lagniappe: Southern Louisiana term meaning a little something extra like a baker's dozen.

Mardi Gras: A large celebration that takes place on Fat Tuesday, the day before Ash Wednesday, the beginning of Lent.

Mince: To chop very fine.

Muffuletta: A sandwich made with seeded buns the size of a dinner plate. It is stuffed with olive salad, meats, and cheeses.

Outlander: A person who is unfamiliar with Cajuns and Cajun country.

Parboil: To boil raw food until it is partially cooked.

Pirogue: A dugout canoe used in the bayou country for fishing, transportation, etc.

Po-Boy: A sandwich on French bread with any and everything on it for a complete meal (see recipe index).

Pot Liquor: The liquid left over after turnip, mustard, and collard greens are cooked. Pour it over cornbread or use for sopping.

Praline: A sweet brown sugar candy mound usually made with pecans.

Ragout (or Fricassee): A thick seasoned stew.

Relish: A highly seasoned food used as an accompaniment.

Roux: A mixture of flour and oil (or tomato paste and oil) cooked at a high temperature until golden or dark brown. It adds great flavor to foods such as Gumbo and Etouffee.

Sauté: To cook in a small amount of fat in a skillet, stirring constantly.

Sear: To burn or char the surface of meat or other foods, usually in hot oil in a skillet or on a hot grill.

Simmer: To cook in a liquid at a temperature just below boiling. Small bubbles form and rise slowly, but the liquid is almost motionless.

Swamp: Wet, spongy land like a bog or marsh.

Tasso: Lean, smoked ham seasoned (coated) with coarse ground black pepper.

RESOURCES

TOURING ACADIANA

The culture of Acadia is very different from the rest of the country and even the State of Louisiana as well. In fact, let's imagine this part of America as a separate state, and it could very well be.

I use James M. Sothern's scenario to depict the state of Acadiana. The state is bounded by the Sabine River on the west the Pearl River on the east, and the Gulf of Mexico on the south. The northern boundary would be a line that runs through Baton Rouge, but would take in L.S.U. and Tiger Stadium. Lafayette would be the state capital. The state flower the Azalea, state tree the live oak, moss draped, of course. State bird the Mallard because this bird is loyal to his mate, is wary, but can be tamed when treated with kindness. They have great pride and affection for their families, and these are traits that are also cherished by Cajun people.

Our flag would have the following symbols: A white banner for honesty and loyalty with a bold cross for Christianity. A Confederate battle flag in the upper right corner for courage and liberty; the Evangeline Oak in the upper left corner would signify patience; the fleur-de-lis in the lower left corner would depict our heritage; and a crawfish in the lower right corner would indicate our love of good food and fellowship.

Folks, these are the traits that Cajuns hold dear. Visit this wonderful state of Acadiana where man hath no gall, and the pace is from yesteryear.

In Acadiana a man's word is his bond and a handshake is usually all the contract you will ever need. *Charley*

ACADIANA, paradise found.

VERMILIONVILLE

Vermilionville (Lafayette) is a 23 acre living history museum celebrating Acadian life with authentic period homes, crafts people, live music, cooking school, restaurant, art gallery and more. It is dedicated to keeping the Acadian culture alive. For more information call 1-800-99-BAYOU or visit http:www.vermillionville.org.

JEAN LAFITTE NATIONAL HISTORICAL PARK AND PRESERVE

The six sites of this historical Park and Preserve were established to preserve significant examples of the natural and cultural resources of Louisiana's Mississippi River Delta region. The sites are: The Prairie Acadian Cultural Center in Eunice, LA (337-262-6862), The Acadian Cultural Center in Lafayette, LA, The Wetlands Acadian Cultural Center in Thibodaux, LA (985-448-1375), The French Quarter in New Orleans, LA (504-589-3882), Barataria Preserve in Marrero, LA (504-589-2330), and Chalmette Battlefield and National Cemetery, Chalmette, LA (504-281-0510). Check them out at www.nps.gov plus the name of the center.

LOUISIANA ATTRACTIONS

Louisianaattractions.com lists many tours, from Sportsman's Paradise to Cross Roads, Cajun Country, Plantations, and New Orleans.

Louisiana Office of Tourism
Tour Guide of Louisiana
Allow 2-4 weeks for delivery
(800) 261-9144 (800) 334-8626

Louisiana Department of Culture, Recreation and Tourism
Office of Tourism,
Inquiry Section
P. O. Box 94291
Baton Rouge, LA 70804-9291
(225) 342-8119 (800) 633-6970

Cajun Country Tour Guide
Featuring South Louisiana's Scenic Byways
Acadian House Publishing
P.O. Box 52247
Lafayette, LA 70505
(337) 235-8851

Abbeville Parish Tourist Commission
P.O. Box 1106
Abbeville, LA 70511-1106
(The Jean Lafitte Scenic Byway)

Acadia Parish Visitors Commission
114 East First Street
Crowley, LA 70527
(337) 783-2108

Breaux Bridge Crawfish Festival
520 Parkway P.O. Box 25
Breaux Bridge, La 70517
(337) 332-6655

Conrad Rice Mill
Home of Konriko Brand
rice products from Louisiana
307 Ann Street
New Iberia, LA 70560
(800) 551-3245

Houma Terrebonne
Tourist Commission
1702 Saint Charles Street
Houma, LA 70360
(Freshwater fishing)
(800) 688-2732

Iberia Parish
Tourist Commission
2704 Hwy. 14
New Iberia, LA 70560
(337) 356-1540

International Petroleum
Museum & Exposition
Known locally as "The Rig
Museum"
Tour offshore oil rig
"Mr. Charlie"
P.O. Box 1988
Morgan City, LA 70380
(985) 384-3744
(call for reservations)

Lafayette Visitor Commission
1400 NW Evangeline Thruway
Lafayette, LA 70501
337-232-3808

Louisiana Association
of Fairs and Festivals
601 Oak Lane
Thibodaux, LA 70301-6537
(985) 446-2132
(send for up to date list)

Louisiana Sugar Cane
Festival
City Park, Parkview Drive
New Iberia, LA 70560
(337) 369-9323

McGee's Landing
in the Atchafalaya Basin
1337 Henderson Levee Blvd.
Henderson, LA 70517
337-228-2384

THE ATCHAFALAYA BASIN

For many generations the Cajuns of the Atchafalaya Basin have depended on this wild and primitive land for their survival. Before the Cajuns it was the home of the Chitimachas Indians who settled this region of the Atchafalaya River. This vast piece of wood lands that covers more than 800,000 acres from Simmesport to Morgan City is one of the most complex man controlled flood systems in the world. It is responsible for draining flood water from as many as 38 of the contiguous United States.

The basin is so dense in many areas, covered with cypress, willow, oak and other species of trees, it became a prime habitat for thousands of species of animals. Deer, rabbit, squirrel, frogs, alligator, turtles, birds and snakes are just a few animals that populate the great basin. Presently millions of pounds of crawfish are harvested in the Atchafalaya Basin by commercial fishermen and exported throughout the world, creating a way for Cajuns to continue making a living by traditional means. *Mark Allemond, a Cajun*

Opelousas Tourism and Activities Committee
P. O. Box 712
Opelousas, LA 70571
800-424-5442

Prairie Acadian Cultural Center
250 W. Park Ave.
Eunice, LA 70535
(337) 457-8490
Part of Jean Lafitte National History

Shadows-on-the-Teche
Tours of Antebellum houses
317 East Main Street
New Iberia, LA 70560

TABASCO Country Store & Visitors Center
Avery Island, LA 70513
(800) 634-9599

Tony Chachere's Cajun & Creole Spices
(Tour famous Cajun spice plant)
544 N. Lombard
Opelousas, LA 70570
(800) 551-9066

Thibodaux Chamber of Commerce
1048 Canal Blvd.
Thibodaux, LA 70301
(985) 446-1187
Fax (985) 446-1191
(Historical churches, sugar plantations, etc.)

Vermillion Village Tours
A Cajun & Creole Living History Museum and Folklife Village
1600 Surrey Street,
P.O. Box 2266
Lafayette, LA 70502-2266
(US) 800-543-5340
(Canada) 800-232-3808

Zydeco Music Festival
457 Zydeco Road,
Suite A
Opelousas, LA 70570
(337) 942-2392

A Cajun Man's Swamp Cruise
3109 Southdown Mandolay
Houma, LA 70360
(985) 868-4625

CAJUN "FUN" TOURS
Serving all Louisiana
701 Parkview Dr.
New Iberia, LA 70560
(337) 369-6777

Honey Island Swamp Tours, Inc.
106 Holly Ridge Dr.
Slidell, LA 70560
(985) 641-1769

Lagniappe Tours
900 North Blvd.
Baton Rouge, LA 70802-5743
(225) 387-2464

RESTAURANTS

We have never had a "bad" meal in Louisiana. There are several places we enjoy and want to share them with you. What we like is, of course delicious prepared cuisine, the proprietors and the ambiance, decor, friendly service, and relaxed atmosphere.

The following lists restaurants we enjoy when we visit Louisiana. Most are in the moderate price range and provides a menu of Cajun and Creole foods that are prepared by the proprietor or professionally trained chefs. Many have decor that have a relaxed atmosphere for family dining. Charley's sister, Margaret Ann, loves to dine at five star Commander's Palace (one of the Brennan family's many restaurants) in New Orleans. It is located on St Charles in the Garden District. We often select the Saturday Jazz Branch at the Commander's Palace when Margaret Ann and husband, Julius Champagne, visit us in New Orleans. We do a biannual stay at our Time share at the Avenue Plaza on St. Charles where we enjoy the Big Easy, and venture into Cajun Land to explore the wonders to be found there.

CAJUN COUNTRY AND CAJUN FAVORITES

Abear's Café (Hebert's Café)
Live Cajun music on weekends
809 Bayou Black Dr.
Houma, LA 70503
985-872-6306

Boudin King Restaurant
906 West Division
Jennings. LA 70546
337-824-6593

Bubba's II Restaurant
and Sports Lounge
Cozy family restaurant on
Bayou Lafourche
764 Bayou Road (Highway 308)
Thibodaux, LA 70301
(985) 446-5117

Café Des Amis
140 E. Bridge St.
Breaux Bridge, LA 70517
(337) 824-5273

Café Manshac
Ray Lyon, renowned Cajun Chef
3822 West Congress

Lafayette, LA 70506
(337) 981-5355

Café Vermilionville
(Housed in an 1800s
Acadian Inn)
1304 W. Pinhook Rd.
Lafayette, LA 70503
(337) 237-0100

Dave's Cajun Cabin
Great Cajun food, owner
managed
6240 West Main
Houma, LA 70360
(504) 868-3870

Don's Seafood Hut
(Since 1934, The Landry Family)
4309 Johnson Street
Lafayette, LA 70508
(337) 981-1141

Dupuy's Oyster shop
Oysters & other Seafood
108 South Main Street
Abbeville, LA 70517

Enola Prudhomme's Cajun Cafe
4676 NE Evangeline Thruway
Carencro, LA 70520
337-824-6593

Landry's Seafood House
I-10 at Louisiana Hwy. 347
Lafayette, LA 70508
(337) 667-6116

Mike Andersons Seafood
1031 West Lee Dr.
Baton Rouge, LA 70808
(225) 766-7823

Mulate's Cajun Restaurant
The Original family restaurant
325 Mills Ave.
Breaux Bridge, LA 70517
1-800-42-Cajun

The Oasis Seafood and Steak
Award winning Cajun cuisine
New Iberia, LA 70560
(337) 369-7022

Pat Huval's Fisherman's Wharf
For over 40 years
P.O. Box 596
Henderson, LA 70521
(337) 228-7110

Poor Boys Riverside Inn
(Finest Cuisine Since 1932)
240 Tubing Road
Lafayette, LA 70508
(337) 837-4011

Prejean's Restaurant
(Seafood, Cajun Band)
34880 U.S. Hwy 167 North
Lafayette, LA 70507
(337) 896-3247

Ralph & Kacoo's
(Cajun and Seafood)
6110 Bluebonnet Road (at I-10)
Baton Rouge, LA 70809
(225) 766-2113

NEW ORLEANS RESTAURANTS
All are great but here are the ones we enjoy.

Acme Oyster and Seafood House
724 Iberville Street
New Orleans. LA 70129
504-522-5973
www.acmeoyster.com
Our favorite for catfish
& oyster Po Boys

Alex Patout's Louisiana
Restaurant
Haute Creole-Cajun Cuisine
221 Royal Street
New Orleans, Louisiana 70130

Café Du Monde
Coffee and Beignets since 1862
800 Decatur Street
New Orleans, Louisiana 70130
They ship coffee and
Beignet mix.
504-772-2927

Casamento's Restaurant
4330 Magazine St.
New Orleans, LA 70115
504-895-9761

Chef's Table Number One
Culinary Institute of New Orleans
2100 Saint Charles Ave.
New Orleans, LA 70140
504-525-2328 chefstable.com

Felix's Oyster Bar and Restaurant
(Where Charley's father taught
him to make Cocktail sauce
in 1948)
210 Bourbon Street, one
block off Canal
New Orleans, LA 70130

KPaul's Louisiana Kitchen
416 Chartres Street
New Orleans, LA 70130
(504) 524-7394

La Crepe Nanou
(A special place for dinner)
1712 Robert St.
New Orleans, LA 70115
(504) 899-2670

Michaul's Live Cajun Music
Restaurant
840 St. Charles Ave.
New Orleans, LA 70130
(504) 523-1709

Mother's
(Po-boys, Red beans and rice)

401 Poydras Street
New Orleans, LA 70130
(504) 523-1620

Smitty's Seafood Restaurant
2000 West Esplanade Ave.
Kenner, LA 70065
(504) 468-1647

The Trolley Café
Where the locals eat;
great for breakfast or lunch
1900 block of St. Charles Ave.
New Orleans, LA 70130

Tujague's Restaurant
(Traditional Creole, started
1856 serving the dock workers,
only Antoine's is older)
(Tell Steve Latter Crazy
Cajun sent you.)
823 Decatur Street
New Orleans, LA 70130
(504) 525-8676

Steamboat Natchez
Nightly Dinner/Jazz cruise
"DUKES OF DIXIELAND"
Depart from JAX Brewery
(800) 233-2628

HOTELS, MOTELS AND BED AND BREAKFASTS

Most of the lodging takes on the flavor of the area. The accommodations you select depend on your personal need and preferences. We belong to the American Automobile Association (AAA) and Quest. These guides classify hotels, motels and some bed and breakfasts and rates them according to the services provided. All lodging listed must meet minimum standards. These guides others help tourists select the services they are comfortable with, they list price ranges to fit within designated budgets, and provide some degree of safety. Always use a reliable source for recommending where you stay. A good lodging in a good section of the town is very important, but not a substitute for common sense. We always stay in New Orleans at the Avenue Plaza on St. Charles. They have wonderful time share studios and one bedroom apartments in one of the best areas in New Orleans, the Garden District.

AAA tour books have a section on guest safety and tips for the traveler which are worth following. Get maps and tour books on Louisiana from your travel or automobile club to help you plan your trip.

When we stay in New Orleans we visit things in New Orleans. Walking tour of historic places and beautiful old homes, self guided tours, museums, the Vieux Carre (French Quarter), riverboat cruises, Ferry boat across the mighty Mississippi to Algiers to visit the Mardi Gras museum, tour: Superdome, St. Louis Cathedral, Aquarium of the Americas, and many museums. Ride the trolley on Saint Charles Ave past the beautiful university campuses of Tulane and Loyola past the Audubon Park, and the Zoological Gardens. Take a 2 hour Cajun or Creole cooking lesson for lunch at the New Orleans School of Cooking in the Jackson Brewery or the Cajun cookin' School in the river walk or?...Best of all, sit and relax on the levee and watch the busy Mississippi working. New Orleans is the most active ports in the United States and is many miles up the Mississippi River from the gulf. Start planning what you want to see and do in New Orleans.

To visit Cajun Country we select larger towns such as Baton Rouge (the capital city, whose name means Red Stick in French), Houma, Thibodaux, Lafayette, Lake Charles or Morgan City, for lodging. We take day trips to see the things of interest to us and have 3-5 days of great adventure. It is going to take many more years for Charley to show me all the things he loves about Louisiana.

Send for your tour guides, and maps and start planning what you want to see in Cajun Country. How about a great festival, swamp tour, drive past large cane fields (Louisiana's agriculture is an over 8 billion dollar industry), bayous, vast swamps, beautiful plantation homes...Don't forget that southwest Louisiana is the land where time forgot, where calendars are used instead of clocks and skyscrapers rise out of the natural splendors of a Sportsman's Paradise bearing witness to Louisiana's vast diversity.

HOTELS AND MOTELS

Check out your favorite hotel or motel; it is probably waiting for you. Use your AAA card and get your discount and confidence that you have the right accommodations. Or check out one of the following places.

Comfort Inn (Just like home)
2445 S. Acadian Thruway
Baton Rouge, LA 70808
(225) 927-5790

Comfort Inn (Everything to
care for yourself)
1421 SE Evangeline Thruway
Lafayette, LA 70501
800-800-8752

Days Inn Lafayette
1620 North University
Lafayette, LA 70506
(800) 329-7466
(Senior discounts)

Holiday Inn
210 S. Hollywood Rd.
Houma, LA 70360
(985) 868-5851

Holiday Inn Jennings
(Full service)
603 Holiday Dr.
Jennings, LA 70546
(337) 824-5280

Hotel Acadiana (Best Western)
1801 West Pinhook Road
Lafayette, LA 70508
(800) 826-8386

Inn on the Bayou
(Waterfront in Historic area)
1101 West Prien Lake Road
Lake Charles, LA 70601
(800) OH-Bayou

Lafayette Hilton & Towers
(Ask for Lagniappe discount)
1521 W. Pinhook Road
Lafayette, LA 70503
(800) 33-Cajun

BED AND BREAKFASTS

Bed and Breakfast Travel
(agent)
8211 Goodwood Blvd.
Baton Rouge, LA 70806
Serving Louisiana and Gulf Coast
(504)923-2337
WWW.BNBTRAVEL.Com
E-Mail BNB@BNBTravel.Com

Aunt Ruby's B & B
(Charming period furniture)
504 Pugo St.
Lake Charles, LA 70601
(337) 430-0603

Capri Court B&B
"Where the bayous come alive"
101 Capri Court, Hwy. 316
Houma, LA 70364
(800) 428-8026

Madewood Plantation
House National Historic
Landmark
4250 Hwy. 308
Napoleonville, LA 70390
(800) 373-7151

Maison Daboval B & B
"Step back in time"
305 E. Louisiana Ave.
Rayne, LA 70578
(337) 334-3489

Sunny Meade B & B
(Our guests are strangers
but once)
230 Topeka Road
Scott, LA 70583
(800) 833-9693

T'Frere's Bed & Breakfast
Charming rooms;
legendary cuisine
Lafayette, LA
(800) 984-9347

MAIL ORDER CATALOGS
(Cajun cuisine; send for catalogs)
Comeaux's Inc.
(Sausages, Boudin, jerky,
fried turkey and 100 other
products)
709 Park Way Dr.
Breaux Bridge, LA 70517
(800) 323-2492
Comeaux.com

Crazy Cajun Enterprises Inc.
"Crazy Charley" Brand Sauces
(Cajun sauce, Gumbo,
Marinade, Chili sauce, Jalapeno

sauce, authentic sauces from
Louisiana, recipes from the
mid-1800s)
877-862-2586
Fax (530) 622-6989
crazy-charley.com

Cannata's (Flavors of Louisiana,
King Cakes, sausage, Cajun Fried
Turkey, pork ribs, hams, coffee,
seasonings, Mardi Gras party
paper goods)
6307 West Park
Houma, LA 70360
1-800-226-6282

WHERE TO GET CAJUN/CREOLE INGREDIENTS
Collected by Chuck Taggart

If you're going to make it yourself, you've got to have the right ingredients. Smoked ham just ain't the same as tasso, those crawfish tails at Gelson's smells ancient and taste worse, and just where the hell do you think you're going to find pickle meat? Well ...

First, you can get a free list of all the seafood processors in the state of Louisiana who ship fresh seafood by calling The Louisiana Seafood Promotion Board in New Orleans at (504) 568-5693. Also, The Louisiana Department of Agriculture in Baton Rouge now has a Crawfish Promotion Board, which can be reached at (504) 922-1280; they have a list of crawfish related business that they'll send upon request. Now, here are a few places I've collected:

MAIL ORDER SOURCES

Battistella's Seafoods
(Fresh and frozen seafood,
all kinds)
1919 Touro Street
New Orleans, LA 70116
(504) 949-2724

Bon Creole Seafood
(Fresh and frozen crawfish
and crawfish fat)
Rt. 3, Box 5180
New Iberia, LA 70560
(337) 229-8397

Bourgeois Meat Market
Meats and Sausages
(Owned and run by the same
family since 1891, make
boudin, andouille, cracklins,
hog's head cheese, smoked
sausage and jerky. Nationwide
shipping.)
543 West Main Street
Thibodaux, LA 70301
(985) 447-7128

Chef John Folse and Company
(Owned and operated by Chef
John Folse, of Lafitte's Landing
fame in Donaldsonville, LA.
Andouille, tasso, smoked
sausage, spicy turkey, etc.)
(800) 256-2433

Crawfish Specialties
(Specializing in all types of craw
fish: live purged, tail meat, soft
shell. Call make sure they're still
shipping.)
Bradley Fuselier
P.O. Box 246
Eunice, LA 70535
(337) 546-0659

Fisherman's Cove
(Mail order supplier for crawfish
tails, tasso, liquid crab boil, Gulf
seafood, and other Louisiana
seafood. Shipped with dry ice or
gel pack.)
3201 Williams Blvd.
Kenner, LA 70065
(800) 443-3474

Fruge Aquafarms
Fresh crawfish and frozen
crawfish tail meat.

Crowley, LA
337-237-0301

Lil' Fisherman
This neighborhood seafood
joint will also pack and
ship seafood, for local
pickups and mail-order;
crawfish in season, oysters,
fresh shrimp, a variety of
fresh fish, plus prepared
etoufee, jambalaya,
gumbo, etc.
3301 Magazine Street
New Orleans, LA
504-897-9907

Louisiana Crawfish Company
They are crawfish farmers and
specialize in the shipment of live
crawfish and fresh or frozen tail
meat throughout the U.S.
Natchitoches, LA
Email jd@lacrawfish.com
(888) 522-7292

Louisiana Seafood Exchange
Boiled and fresh seafood
504-834-9393

Pearl Brand Shrimp
(Pearl Brand Shrimp serves the
restaurant and wholesale indus
try with quality shrimp for 75
years. Now, we accept retail
orders for our cooked and
fresh frozen shrimp for
customers in the United
States and Canada.)
Indian Ridge Shrimp Company
Houma, LA 70360
(800) 594-0920

Randol's Seafood
(South Louisiana seafood)
Lafayette, LA
(800) YO-CAJUN

Tony's Seafood Market
Fresh seasonal seafood shipped
nationwide. Bulk spices and
seasonings.
5215 Plank Road
Baton Rouge, LA 70805
(225) 357-9669

Li'l Sal's Seafood
Delivery anywhere
1100 24th Street
Kenner, LA 70062
877-541-3524
Fax 775-255-1712
li'lsalseafood.com

Jacob's World Famous Andouille
Also serving hog's head cheese;
boudin, tasso, smoked sausage,
fresh sausage, smoked chicken
and more. "Your satisfaction is
always guaranteed." In the
"Andouille Capital of the World."
505 West Airline Hwy.
La Place, LA 70068
877-215-7589
cajunsausage.com

K-Pauls Cajun Sausages
Andouille, tasso, home of Cajun
Magic spices by Chef Paul
Prudhomme
800-654-6017

Poche's Market
Gumbo Pages reader and Baton
Rouge expert Randy Wright
reports: "They ship great made
on site goodies. Cracklin, boudin,
andouille, tasso, and the best
fresh chaurice on the planet. The
smoked is good, but get the fresh
and grill it with some nice vegetables and a little black beans.
You'll drive Southern California
inta da swamps wit dis one, man.
It also will put an incredible
creamy mouth on a gumbo if
added about 20 minutes from
serving. The chaurice is sold in 10
pound minimum, and you can
mix products."
3015-A Main Hwy.
Breaux Bridge. LA 70517
337-332-2108
Fax 337-332-5051

Other Louisiana Food Products: Spices, Rice, Hot Sauces, Coffee, King Cakes, etc.

Café Du Monde
The original French Market
coffee
Home of the Beignet—French
Doughnut
Coffee with chicory, beignet mix
1039 Decatur Street
New Orleans, LA 70116
800-772-2927

The Cajun Grocer
These folks say they're the first,
secure e-commerce site featuring Louisiana products: food,
music cookbooks, recipes from
Marcelle Bienvenu (their execu-
tive food editor), plus fresh prepared foods, such as boudin,
stuffed chickens, marinated

pork chops, gumbo, etc.
cajungrocer.com

Cajun Injector by Chef Williams
(For everyone looking to stick a
needle into your about-to-be-
deep-fried turkey or other meats
to inject it with something tasty.
Bruce Foods
(337)-365-8101

Central Grocery
The creators of the world
famous Muffuletta. Mail-order
Muffulettas, olive salad,
and more.
French Quarter
New Orleans.
504-523-1620

Community Coffee
New Orleans-style dark roast
coffee and chicory. The quintes
sential Louisiana coffee, now
available by mail-order.
800-535-5583

Gambino's Bakery
Your King Cake headquarters.
They offer king cakes in several
sizes and flavors, and ship to
most locations nationwide.
800-gambino

Haydel's Bakery
King cakes for Carnival season.
800-442-1342

Konriko Rice Products
Rice products and more
800-551-3245
conradricemill.com
New Orleans School of Cooking
and Louisiana General Store in

the Jax Brewery
Their catalogue has about 30
pages of just about everything—
spices, seasonings, hot sauces,
even kitchen equipment.
Muffuletta alert! You can mail
order Central Grocery Olive
Salad from these folks—maybe
not the cheapest.
French Quarter
(800) 237-4841

Progress Grocery
An Italian grocery and muffuletta
shop in the Quarter, brought to
you by three generations of the
Perrone family. Mail order
muffulettas, olive salad, and
many more Italian, Creole and
Cajun ingredients.
French Quarter
(504) 525-6627

Stansel Rice Company
(Home of Ellis Stansel's
Popcorn Rice, grown in
Louisiana and one of my
favorite kinds of rice.)
Gueydan, Louisiana

Steen's 100% Pure Cane Syrup
(The products of C. S. Steen's
Syrup Mill have since 1910 been
a staple in many Louisiana
recipes. On their site you'll find
mail order info, history, and
recipes.)
Abbeville, Louisiana

Zapp's Potato Chips
Louisiana potato chips, and the
best! "Cajun Craw-tators" (sort
of a spicy seafood-boil flavor),
jalapeno, mesquite BBQ, dill,

sour cream and Creole onion, honey-mustard (yum!), regular and salt-free. Plus red bean dip, t-shirts, etc.
Gramercy, LA 70052-1533
(800) HOT-CHIP

Zatarain's
The premier manufacturer of New Orleans seasonings and spices, plus mixes for things like gumbo, jambalaya, etc. Buy them at your local grocery.

In Southern California (for Louisiana Expatriates in L.A.-L.A. land)

The New Orleans Fish Market
Fresh seafood from Louisiana, including crawfish (in season), blue crabs, hot sausage, smoked sausage, tasso, pickle meat, plus prepared bisque and etouffee to go. Also po-boy bread, Camellia red beans, cane syrup ... just about everything you need!
2212 W. Vernon,
corner of Arlington
Los Angeles, CA
(323) 298-9738

Pete's Hot Links
(Fantastic Louisiana-style fresh hot sausage, practically the best in town, next to the late Mr. Jase's homemade hot sausage at Sid's Cafe.)
3701 W. Jefferson near Crenshaw
(323) 735-7470

European Deluxe
Sausage Kitchen
(The gentlemen who run this little establishment are, I

believe, Swiss, and in addition to the many European meats and sausages they offer, they also make a wonderful Louisiana andouille.)
9109 W. Olympic
Beverly Hills, CA
(310) 276-1331

You can also try the Grand Central Market in downtown L.A. for seafood, including live blue crabs.

Crawfish Line (Shipped live-crawfish for your crawfish boil. Boil them in your backyard in a large pot with a stainless steel basket for ease of removing them, cover, boil 7 minutes, make sure crawfish sink. Push them down into boiling water, add crab boil, small new pota-toes, lemon, and white onions to the boiling water. Invite lots of happy people.)
Breaux Bridge, LA
(800) 272-9347 (800-Crawfish)

Web Sites:

Where to send for Crazy Charley brand products:

Clubsauce.com
Concord, CA

Cosmichile.com
Bozeman, MT
406-582-0920

SalsaExpress.com
Fredericksburg, TX
(800) 437-2572

crazy-charley.com
California
(877) 862-2586

tastygifts.com
Houston, TX
(877) 606-7519

RECOMMENDED COOKBOOKS

Bayou Civic Club. *DOWN THE Bayou* (collection of favorite recipes). Larose, La.: Bayou Civic Club, 1985.

Better Homes and Gardens. *Cajun Cooking*. Des Moines: Meredith, 1989.

Chance, Jeanne Lousie Duzant. *Ma Chances' French Caribbean Creole Cooking*. New York: G. P. Putnam's Sons, 1985.

Collin, Rima and Richard. *The New Orleans Cookbook (Creole, Cajun and Louisiana French Recipes Past and Present)*. New York: Alfred A. Knopf, 1987.

Junior League of Lafayette. *TALK ABOUT GOOD!* Lafayette, La: Junior League of Lafayette, 1992. (Recipes contributed by Members of the Lafayette Junior League, their relatives and friends.)

Maring, Margaret. *Louisiana CREOLE & CAJUN*. Boynton Beach, Fla.: American Cooking Guild, 1985 Revised edition 1997, (800) 367-9388.

McIlhenny, Paul, with Barbara Hunter. *The Tabasco Brand Cookbook (125 Years of America's Favorite Pepper Sauce)*. New York: Clarkson Potter, 1993.

Prudhomme, Enola. *Low-Calorie Cajun Cooking*. New York: Hearst, 1991.

Prudhomme, Paul. *Chef Paul Prudhomme's Louisiana Kitchen*. New York: Morrow, 1984.

———. *Fork in the Road*. New York: Morrow, 1993.

———. *PURE MAGIC*. New York: Morrow, 1995.

Prudhomme, Paul, and the Eleven Prudhomme Brothers and Sisters. *The PRUDHOMME Family Cookbook*. New York: Morrow, 1987.

Wilson, Justin. *The Justin Wilson Cook Book*. Gretna, La.: Pelican, 1991.

———. *The Justin Wilson #2 Cook Book: Cookin' Cajun*. Gretna, La.: Pelican, 1979.

RECOMMENDED READINGS

ACADIANA PROFILE MAGAZINE (quarterly). Acadian News Agency,

P.O. Box 52247, Lafayette, LA 70505. Published since 1969 it covers a wide range of interesting facts, tales, recipes, history, personalities, festivals, contests, fishing, music, pictures and inspiration about Cajuns and Cajun country.

Acadiana Profile, 1997. *Cajun Country Tour Guide*. Acadian House Publishing, P.O. Box 52247, Lafayette, LA 70505. This book is designed to help you find your way around Cajun Country, lots of maps, color photography, and write us on 280 points of interest.

Angers, Trent, 1990. *The Truth about the Cajuns*. Acadian House of Publishing, P.O. Box 52247, Lafayette, LA 70505. Trent Angers, editor of "Acadiana Profile" The magazine of the Cajun Country, was encouraged by many to write this book. Disturbed by the way Cajuns were being portrayed in the media nationally, he wanted to set the record straight. This book, a pleasure to read, reflects how truly proud the Cajuns are of their Acadian heritage.

cajunland.com. Best source for anything in and around Louisiana.

cajungrocer.com for any Cajun grocery item.

Fry, Macon, and Julie Posner, 1993. *Cajun Country Guide*. Pelican Publishing Co., Gretna, LA. A comprehensive directory to the sights, sounds, and flavors of Cajun Country.

Ruston, William Faulkner, 1979. *The Cajuns from Acadia to Louisiana*. The Noonday Press, Farrar, Straus and Giroux, New York, New York. An accurate account of the people known as "Cajuns". It is a mix of history and contemporary life and lore about Louisiana's Cajuns.

Saxon, Lyle, Edward Dreyer and Robert Tallant, 1991. *Gumbo Ya-Ya*. Pelican Publishing Company, Gretna, LA. A delightful collection of Louisiana folk tales of the various racial groups, sponsored by the Louisiana State Library Commission.

West, Robert C. 1986. *Atlas of Louisiana Surnames of French and Spanish Origin*. Geoscience Publication, Baton Rouge, LA. Author is a professor emeritus of geography at Louisiana State University (LSU) in Baton Rouge. This atlas covers the 100 most common French and Spanish names and features map showing the concentration of each family in Southern LA. Hebert (pronounced Abear) is the largest French family in Louisiana.

Wilson, Justin, and Howard Jacobs. *Justin Wilson's Cajun Humor.* Pelican Publishing Company, Gretna, LA, 1974 (fifth printing 1991). Justin Wilson was a great spinner of Cajun tales.

INDEX OF RECIPES

INDEX OF STORIES